GLOUCESTER RUGBY CLUB

A
CHERRY AND WHITES
COMPANION

Gloucester R.F.C. team photograph from the 1904-1905 season

GLOUCESTER RUGBY CLUB

A
CHERRY AND WHITES
COMPANION

A miscellany of fantastic facts in A-Z sequence

DAVID KING

AMBERLEY

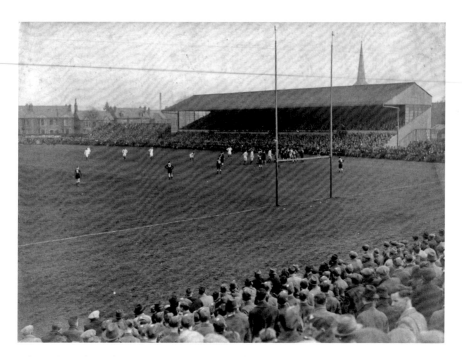

Gloucester play at Kingsholm in an early home fixture

First published 2009

Amberley Publishing
Cirencester Road, Chalford,
Stroud, Gloucestershire, GL6 8PE

www.amberley-books.com

British Library Cataloguing in Publication Data.
A catalogue record for this book is available from the British Library.

ISBN 978 1 84868 865 0
Typesetting and Origination by Amberley Publishing.
Printed in Great Britain.

FOREWORD

It was in the late 1940s that I entered Kingsholm for the first time as a small lad taken by his father at Yuletide. Yes, it was Christmas, for in those days sport was a priority on Christmas Day and Boxing Day. It was tradition that Old Merchant Taylors and University Athletics Union were the annual visitors to Kingsholm.

Kingsholm, in those far off days was a totally different stadium to the one we behold today. The game of Rugby Union was different, amateur, slower and, whisper it quietly, a tad rougher.

Thousands have watched the 'Cherry and Whites,' since it was founded or should we say Gloucester Rugby Football Club, nay in modern day language – Gloucester Rugby! To many neither applies, for the majority it will always be 'Cherry and Whites'. Commercial reasons apart the die hards will always hold sway.

A 'Cherry and White' fan is proud of his team. A bond that a lot of clubs would like to experience. The Kingsholm experience is a factor to behold. Friends and relations flock to the stadium on match days, they all have common ground. Of course over the decades there have been many converted to the game due to the coverage associated with Sky TV and to a lesser extent terrestrial television.

This book is written in the hope that it will bring the reader a little knowledge and even closer to the Club. The game of Rugby Union, and especially the clubs, have suffered from a dearth of books on the subject. Hopefully, this volume will deal with fact and not fiction, enabling records to be there for posterity.

Glorious Gloucester, originally a fort and still a major junction as it was in Roman times – *Glevum*. The city is famous for its eleventh-century cathedral and its twenty-first century Rugby Union club. Both are majestic and seemingly impregnable over the years and decades. May that fact be preserved.

David King

ACKNOWLEDGEMENTS

My grateful thanks to the following who have helped me in no small measure in producing this book – Sally Jones, Carole Elkins, Tim Holder, John Hudson, and Andy Davey for his excellent caricatures.

Gloucester storm home

THESE are conceivably the most heady days that English rugby has known and we duly had a packed and thrilled Twickenham, which watched four excellent Powergen finals at various levels and which positively basked in a stunning final of verve, movement and controversy, after which the glorious gladiators of Gloucester had won a resounding victory.

Their authority grew and grew throughout the game, the scenes of delirium at the end could hardly have been bettered at the old ground and, frankly, Northampton were simply blasted out of the contest.

Gloucester's third cup victory was sealed in a grand but rather ironic manner in Dublin last weekend, had struggled all day with his own fatigue and against the crushing superiority of the Gloucester pack and he tried one final flicked pass to try to drag back an 11-point deficit as time ran out. However, Ludovic Mercier, vastly influential for Gloucester, intercepted the pass and set off with 90m to go. He did not have the pace to go the whole way, but he knew a man who did. James Simpson-Daniel came cruising up alongside and unleashed a devastating burst for the line.

Gloucester's recent history has been rather clouded by the financial problems of Tom Walkinshaw, their owner, in his ill-starred Formula One career. If Walkinshaw's heart is truly in the club, then he will surely end any uncertainty by reaffirming his financial commitment and releasing the various financial streams; or if not, he must sell to someone who can.

Certainly, he has a wonderful institution on his hands. Gloucester's pack, with Olivier Azam and the astounding James Forrester on rampaging form, eventually played the heart out of Northampton and, behind the scrum, it was hardly a contest either.

It was hard on Northampton's international giants to expect them to reproduce their top form so soon after the Grand Slam, but at least Northampton played their full part in a stunningly atmospheric occasion, set off earlier in the afternoon by another blistering final between Orrell and Exeter.

Gloucester were trailing 3-0 when they scored their first try and, ironically, it was a try coughed up by two of England's premier heroes. Northampton won the ball in their own 22, Matt Dawson tried to whip it away to Steven Thompson, but the big England hooker

allowed the ball to pass in front of him, and Simpson-Daniel reacted with real alacrity to follow up and score. That is what comes of having hookers, even richly talented ones, standing in at fly-half.

Ludovic Mercier extended the lead to 10-3 with a lovely high drop-goal, but Gloucester fell foul of Mr Spreadbury when Rob Fidler was sent to the sin-bin for an offence in a ruck. First, it seemed that Northampton would take a heavy toll. Paul Grayson kicked his second and third penalties and then cut past Mercier in startling style, and found the powerful Nick Beal inside him. Beal set off on an arcing scoring run and Grayson's conversion made it 16-10, with Fidler still fuming in the

bin. However, he soon felt a good deal better.

Thimus Delport attacked powerfully down the left and, when Gloucester switched the play, James Forrester sold a flourishing dummy, burst between Thompson and Robbie Morris, drew the cover defence and sent the speeding Marcel Garvey over for a remarkable try.

The rest of the half, sadly, was a testimony to the referee's ability to spot the most finicky semi-infringements, and two penalties by Grayson sent Northampton in at 22-20 the good after a half worth anybody's money.

The rags to riches nature of proceedings continued at the start of the second half, not to mention the quality of the

rugby. Gloucester were now clearly enjoying an edge in the forward play and they burst into the lead again with another stirring try.

They sent long passes to attack the two sides of the pitch in turn and, after a final switch, long passes from Mercier and Henry Paul took play back toward the right. Garvey batted Paul's pass on under pressure, the remarkable Forrester popped up near the right wing and made a typically devastating burst to score. The replays showed that he had not grounded the ball properly, although it was the sort of score which is always given.

Gloucester may have been unfortunate soon afterwards as they returned to the attack when two Northampton players collided and Beal clearly threw the ball deliberately into touch. The referee, equally clearly, indicated a penalty to Gloucester but, after absorbing a barrage of advice and criticism from Northampton during a break for injury, he had reduced the award to a mere scrum, so Gloucester led 27-22 as the matched moved into the final quarter.

Almost the entire second half was played in Northampton's territory and, indeed, there were a fair number of opportunities

for Gloucester to finally bury the struggling Saints.

Their struggles multiplied after the hour with one of those nonsensical sin-binnings without which modern day referees begin to fret. Grayson was running back to tackle Paul, the flight of the ball towards Paul was obscured and Grayson brushed his man early before the charging Paul gained possession.

It was clearly a penalty but, to send Grayson to the bin for what was nothing more than an instinctive reaction was ridiculous, and, by the time Grayson returned inside the last four minutes, Mercier had kicked two more penalties to take Gloucester almost out of range. The trophy was theirs.

Gloucester: T Delport; M Garvey, T Fanolua, H Paul (R Todd 74min), J Simpson-Daniel; L Mercier, A Gomarsall; T Woodman, O Azam, A Deacon, A Eustace, R Fidler, J Boer (capt), J Paramore 26-37min), J Forrester, A Hazell (J Paramore 60min, E Pearce 74min).

Northampton: N Beal; B Reihana, P Jorgensen (C Hyndman 63min), J Leslie (co-capt), B Cohen; P Grayson, M Dawson; T Smith, S Thompson, R Morris (M Stewart 53min), M Lord, S Williams (D Fox 76min), M Connors, A Blowers, B Pountney (co-capt).

Yellow cards: Gloucester: Fidler (22min), Delport (79min). **Northampton:** Grayson (64min).

Gloucester 40
Tries: Simpson-Daniel (2), Garvey, Forrester. Conversions: Mercier (4). Penalties: Mercier, (3) Drop Goal: Mercier

Northampton 22
Try: Beal. Conversion: Grayson
Penalties: Grayson (5)

Referee: A Spreadbury (RFU), Attendance: 75,000

Stephen Jones at Twickenham

PREFACE

This book has been compiled as a miscellany of facts, stats and fascinating notes from the Club's distant past and recent seasons, arranged in A-Z sequence.

A smattering of black and white images have been added throughout the book for the reader's amusement, though these do not necessarily relate the the A-Z sequence.

Gloucester seeking to end 20-year final drought

Fans' power is key to cup bid

GLOUCESTER coach John Brain is appealing to his team's supporters to roar the players to victory in the Cheltenham and Gloucester Cup final tonight (kick-off 8pm).

Gloucester are taking on Allied Dunbar Premiership Two leaders Bedford in the first final of the new competition at Northampton. Both clubs have sold around 2,500 tickets for the match and Brain wants the Gloucester faithful to out shout the Blues' fans.

"The first 20 minutes and the last 20 minutes will be very important," said Brain, who has been in charge of the Gloucester team this week with director of coaching Richard Hill away on England A duty.

"You always need to get a good start at neutral grounds. We are glad there is plenty of support going because the idea is to make that neutral ground as much your own ground as possible.

"We will be trying to turn it into a home match. The last 20 minutes will be important too, but they are important in any game."

Gloucester have not been in a 15-a-side cup final since losing to Bath at Twickenham in 1990 and they last won a cup final outright in 1978 when they beat Leicester.

This new Cheltenham and Gloucester Cup does not have the prestige of the Tetley's Bitter Cup, but Gloucester are still keen to win and bring home the trophy and the £20,000 winner's cheque instead of the £10,000 prize for the losing finalists.

by Katie Coker

"League rugby is very, very important and even the Tetley's Bitter Cup is reducing in importance slightly," said Brain. "But the attitude of the players is that we have got to the final and Gloucester haven't won anything on the 15-a-side rugby front for years, so we want to do well.

"We know what we are up against. We under-performed against Bedford when they beat us in February.

"But if we had under-performed that badly against one of the top four or five sides we would have conceded 50 points, and we only conceded 32.

"They are a good side, but I don't think we saw anything from them to be afraid of."

Gloucester travelled to Northampton this morning and spent the day at a hotel so the players could rest and prepare for the game together.

"There is always that bit of apprehension among the players – Gloucester aren't used to being in cup finals," said Brain.

"Everyone is a bit anxious about how we are going to perform and the mental preparation is the key. We have to relax and be confident."

● See page 61 for more news.

■ Scott Benton . . . hoping to win his first England cap at Twickenham tomorrow. See story below.

Scrum down during a 2005 fixture against Saracens

A

ADAM

He may not have been the first man on earth but Adam Eustace was the first professional player with the forename of Adam to play for the Club. He made his debut for Gloucester on 27th March 1999 versus Bedford at Goldington Road in a 19-15 defeat. Adam left Gloucester R.F.C. in May 2007 to join Llanelli Starlets but rejoined the Club for the 2008-09 season.

ADAM BALDING

Another player with the famous forename joined the Club from Leicester Tigers in June 2004. Adam, made his debut for Gloucester Rugby Club on 5th September 2004 versus Leeds at Headingly. Ironically, he joined Leeds Carnegie on a three month loan deal in December 2007 and eventually joined Newcastle Falcons in 2008. Adam, is currently on the playing staff of Newcastle Falcons.

AGAINST

The following clubs have provided opposition during the course of the Club's history, all the names beginning with the letter A:

Aberavon, Abertillery, Army, A. C. Wellington, Ashford House, Auckland, Agen.

ALONE

Anthony Allen is the only player from the Club to be capped by England with the surname beginning with the letter A, his forename also. Anthony was born on 1ˢᵗ September 1986 at Southampton. He made his debut for England on 5ᵗʰ November 2006 versus New Zealand at Twickenham. The famous All Blacks inflicted a resounding 41 points to twenty defeat upon the host country.

ATTENDANCE

The highest attendance at Kingsholm which created a new Club record in the professional era is 16,500 which is the capacity at Kingsholm. Matches with Bath and Bristol in the seasons of 2000/2008 and 2008/2009 have reached the maximum. Attendances have varied with some higher at the 'Spa' the Club's first ground than at their present Kingsholm ground on occasions. The visit of Munster on 5ᵗʰ April 2008 attracted a maximum of 16,500.

ASHTON GATE

Due to ground reconstruction at Kingsholm the Guinness League fixture with Bristol on 28ᵗʰ April 2007 was played at Ashton Gate, the home of Bristol City Football Club. Although staged in the City of Bristol there was a favourable outcome with a 35-13 victory ensuing. There was an attendance of 15,852.

OLIVIER AZAM

The French International hooker Olivier Azam became the first overseas player in the professional era at Kingsholm with his surname commencing with 'A'. He made his debut for the Club on 3ʳᵈ September 2001 versus Saracens at Vicarage Road, Watford. Jack Adams and Anthony Allen followed suit with Simon Amor who joined London Wasps in 2007, therefore completing a quartet.

ALOFT

John A' Bear is the only player with the initial 'A' to have captained the Club. John captained the Club in the 1937-38 and 1938-39 seasons.

ADAM AND ANDREW

Adam Eustace and Andrew Hazell are the only two players to have been Cup winners with their forenames commencing with the letter 'A'. Both players appeared in the 2003 Powergen Cup triumph at Twickenham against Northampton Saints on Saturday 5th April 2003. The Kick-Off was at 4.30 p.m.

ARNOLD ALCOCK

Arnold Alcock a former President of Gloucester Rugby Club was awarded an England International Cap by mistake. The incident occurred in 1906 when the England selectors in a clerical error sent a letter intended for Liverpool's Lancelot Slocock to Arnold by mistake. He represented Guys Hospital at the time and appeared against South Africa. Arnold never played for England again. Laurence Slocock went on to later represent his country in eight Internationals. Arnold was born on 18th August 1882 in Woolstanton, Staffordshire. He passed away on 7th November 1973 in Gloucester.

AMATEUR ERA

The sport of Rugby Union stayed as an amateur game until the professional era was initiated in 1996.

ALBERT MEDAL

The Albert Medal was awarded to Christopher Champion Tanner in the Second World War. He forfeited his life in saving others when HMS *Fiji* was torpedoed off the Island of Crete on 23rd May 1941 when the Island was being evacuated.

NATIONAL CUP WINNER – A

Olivier Azam.

AWAY – EUROPE

The Club's first away match in European Competition was played at St Helens, Swansea on 19th October 1996 when a heavy defeat was inflicted by the Welsh club by 62 points to twelve.

AWAY – LEAGUE

The most points recorded in an away League match was the 50 points scored versus Leeds on 12th May 2002.

AGAINST – AT HOME

The most points conceded at Kingsholm in a League match were the 40 points scored by Leicester in the 2001-02 season in the Zurich Premiership.

AGAINST – AWAY

The most points conceded in an away League encounter was the 76 recorded by Harlequins on 31st August 1996 in Courage League I.

AGAIN AND AGAIN

The most tries scored in a league match was the eleven recorded versus Sale on 16th April 1988.

AWAY – OH DEAR!

Eleven tries have been conceded twice, versus Harlequins on 31st August 1996 and versus Bath on 30th April 1997, both in Courage League I fixtures.

ANNUAL

The Club Annual General Meeting in 1884 agreed to pay players travel and hotel expenses for away matches.

ATTENDANCES

How attendances have risen at Kingsholm! In 1996-97 the average attendance for league matches was a mere 4,963.

ATTENDING THE ANNUAL

The first Annual General Meeting of the Club was held at the Spread Eagle Hotel on 3rd October 1894 where it was reported to those attending that Gloucester Football Club was in a prosperous condition.

ADIDAS

Adidas were the first club sponsors in 1976 providing free kit for players and boots at a reduced price. In that same year Match Sponsors and perimeter advertising generated £5,000 per season.

ANGLO-WELSH

The Anglo-Welsh League with seventeen clubs participating was introduced in 1976. It was disbanded two years later and replaced by the Rugby Football Union merit table.

AUSTRALIANS

Three Australian Internationals have played for Gloucester – Jason Little, Jeremy Paul and Richard Tombs. While another Australian to appear for the Club has been Duncan McCrae.

APPEARANCES

Top Five Record Appearances:

Alan Brinn	572	Dick Smith	540
Bob Clewes	521	Peter Ford	506
Richard Mogg	501		

ATTENDANCES

Attendances at the Spa were reduced by fifty percent in the 1888-89 season due to the Boer War conflict and a smallpox epidemic within the city.

ADVERTS

Adverts of forthcoming matches were placed in the local newspaper in the nineteenth century regarding fixtures at The Spa.

ACTUAL ATTENDANCE

Just 10,500 turned up to watch the first final of England clubs knockout cup in 1972 between Gloucester R.F.C. and Moseley R.F.C at Twickenham. In 1978 24,000 watched Gloucester defeat Leicester 6 points to three at Twickenham.

ANGLO-WELSH

The club became the Anglo Welsh pennant champions in the 1981/82 season as well as joint winners of the John Player Cup. A season in which Gloucester R.F.C. set a new record for wins in a season – 41 from 48 fixtures played.

AMOR

Former Gloucester Rugby Club scrum half, Simon Amor, captained the England Sevens team to the Hong Kong title and to a silver medal in the 2006 Commonwealth Games in Melbourne, Australia.

AZAM – AGAIN

Gloucester Rugby Club hooker Olivier Azam was a European Challenge Cup winner with Montferrand in 1999. 'Olly' played in the 35-16 win over Bourgoin at Stade Gerland in Lyon in front of 31,986. He was Man of the Match when Montferrand lost 27-26 to N.E.C. Harlequins at the Madejski Stadium in 2004 in the same competition.

AGGREGATES AND AVERAGES IN LEAGUE MATCHES AT KINGSHOLM

	AGGREGATE	AVERAGE
2001-2002	103,547	9,413
2002-2003	115,968	10,542
2003-2004	117,929	10,720
2004-2005	136,700	12,427
2005-2006	131,253	11,932
2006-2007	118,165	11,816
If the Ashton Gate match is included		
2007-2008	134,017	12,183
2007-2008	153,998	13,999
2008-2009	157,280	14,298

AGGREGATES AND AVERAGES AT KINGSHOLM IN EUROPE

SEASON	COMPETITION	AGGREGATE	AVERAGE
1997-1998	European Conference	13,008	4,336
1999-2000	European Shield	9.597	3,193
2000-2001	Heineken Cup	31,325	6,265
2001-2002	European Shield	27,287	6,821
2002-2003	Heineken Cup	27,303	9,127
2003-2004	Heineken Cup	31,209	10,403
2004-2005	Heineken Cup	37,282	12,427
2005-2006	European Challenge Cup	41,932	8,386
2006-2007	Heineken Cup	32,383	10,794
2007-2008	Heineken Cup	57,576	14,394
2008-2009	Heineken Cup	78,450	13,075

DAVID AINGE

The Gloucester full back scored 153 points for the Club in the 1966/67 season then left the Club to join Bristol and became the first player to record 100 points in September in Rugby history. David later rejoined Gloucester R.F.C. for a second spell.

ATHLETICALLY ADEPT – MUSICAL TOO

Former Gloucester Rugby Football Club fullback George Romans played County Cricket for Gloucestershire; he also represented Gloucester City at hockey, water polo, tennis and played soccer for the Gloucester Thursday team. He also represented the City at athletics. He was also with the Gloucester Operatic Society. George, who played for St Georges and Barnwood, captained the 'City' club as this Club was known from 1901 to 1905. He represented the County and played in International trials. He later became a referee and took control of a semi-final in the County Championship. George made 268 first team appearances, scoring 7 tries, converting 352, kicking 24 penalties and recording 6 drop goals.

AVERAGES

Those players who have represented Gloucester Rugby Football Club and also played Cricket at first class level for Gloucestershire County Cricket Club have career averages as follows for the County:

	Matches	Innings	Not Out	Runs	Highest	Average Score
H. J. Boughton 1884-1888	7	12	2	114	41	11.40
M. H. Cullimore 1929	3	3	0	19	15	6.33
G. L. Jessop 1894-1914	345	605	23	18,936	286	32.53
M. A. McCanlis 1929	1	0	0	0	0	0
H. V. Page 1883-1895	102	165	16	2358	116	18.70
G. W. Parker 1932-1950	70	112	9	1954	210	18.97
G. Romans 1899-1903	11	19	3	218	62	13.62

APRIL ABANDONMENT

On Saturday April 22nd 1922 the Club announced that the following season's fixture with Leicester had been cancelled. This step was taken following correspondence arising out of the appointment of the referee for the match on March 25th of that year.

Leicester's complaint was that they wanted a Major Wilkins of London instead of J. H. Burge of Somerset who they considered not to be impartial!

ARGENTINIAN INTERNATIONALS

Diego Albanese and Rodrigo Roncero have appeared for Gloucester R.F.C. Diego later joined Leeds and Rodrigo moved to Stade Francais in Paris.

AWARDS ABOUND

The Club's former French prop forward Christian Califano who played for five clubs during his playing career – Bourges, Stade Toulousian, Auckland Blues, S. V. Agen, Saracens and Gloucester had his own personal honours board.

Christian, twice won the Five Nations Grand Slam with France in 1997 and 1998. He won the French Championship with Stade Toulousain in 1994, 1995, 1996, 1999 and 2001. Still with Stade Toulousain he added the European Cup in 1996, the French National Cup in 1998, the Challenge Yves du Manoir (1993) and Coupe Latine 1995 and 1997. Christian became the first French front row player to score a hat trick of tries in an International when he did so versus Romania in 1996. In an International career that spanned from 1994 to 2007 he was awarded 71 caps scoring 6 tries. His first cap was against New Zealand and they were also the opponents when he made his last International appearance in 2007.

AWAY MATCHES WON – 1891-2008

	PLAYED	WON	DREW	LOST	POINTS FOR	POINTS AGAINST
1891-1892	10	5	1	4	66	56
1892-1893	11	5	1	5	53	89
1893-1894	10	5	0	5	53	105

	PLAYED	WON	DREW	LOST	POINTS FOR	POINTS AGAINST
1894-1895	9	2	2	5	45	69
1895-1896	10	3	2	5	30	67
1896-1897	13	5	3	5	76	86
1897-1898	16	10	2	4	126	91
1898-1899	13	9	1	3	83	39
1899-1900	14	9	1	4	169	69
1900-1901	14	7	3	4	176	52
1901-1902	12	8	1	3	138	34
1902-1903	17	7	1	9	105	116
1903-1904	15	6	2	7	146	88
1904-1905	15	6	0	9	135	106
1905-1906	13	6	2	5	83	58
1906-1907	15	6	2	7	77	135
1907-1908	12	2	2	8	53	110
1908-1909	15	9	0	6	155	117
1909-1910	15	4	5	6	93	109
1910-1911	20	9	1	10	117	116
1911-1912	19	8	1	10	103	117
1912-1913	17	6	1	10	84	138
1913-1914	16	7	1	8	91	107
1919-1920	15	7	1	7	171	115
1920-1921	16	6	0	10	159	169
1921-1922	18	6	1	11	128	237
1922-1923	18	8	1	9	184	157
1923-1924	18	7	0	11	103	174
1924-1925	16	7	0	9	107	146
1925-1926	15	5	0	10	130	122
1926-1927	15	2	0	13	83	197
1927-1928	17	6	3	8	112	129
1928-1929	18	6	2	10	129	151
1929-1930	19	8	1	10	151	150
1930-1931	18	6	3	9	112	171
1931-1932	13	1	2	10	41	116
1932-1933	16	7	3	6	105	121
1933-1934	15	8	1	6	114	98
1934-1935	15	5	0	10	88	183
1935-1936	16	8	3	5	114	103
1936-1937	13	6	1	6	72	98
1937-1938	14	9	1	4	127	120

	PLAYED	WON	DREW	LOST	POINTS FOR	POINTS AGAINST
1938-1939	16	5	3	8	109	153
1939-1940	3	0	0	3	16	47
1945-1946	10	5	3	2	129	116
1946-1947	11	3	0	8	58	102
1947-1948	20	11	1	8	238	183
1948-1949	19	5	2	12	117	172
1949-1950	20	7	2	11	110	166
1950-1951	16	4	2	10	71	118
1951-1952	19	9	2	8	157	158
1952-1953	18	5	2	11	121	167
1953-1954	17	10	1	6	155	122
1954-1955	16	5	0	11	140	196
1955-1956	20	4	1	15	112	221
1956-1957	18	8	1	9	131	179
1957-1958	18	8	2	8	135	160
1958-1959	15	5	1	9	76	152
1959-1960	21	10	1	10	200	193
1960-1961	17	3	2	12	95	167
1961-1962	21	6	2	13	175	279
1962-1963	16	6	0	10	120	174
1963-1964	20	11	2	7	209	143
1964-1965	19	6	1	12	132	289
1965-1966	22	8	3	11	132	179
1966-1967	21	4	3	14	112	298
1967-1968	25	9	2	14	230	232
1968-1969	19	9	3	7	224	248
1969-1970	24	9	0	15	239	378
1970-1971	21	8	2	11	177	191
1971-1972	26	15	2	9	332	244
1972-1973	25	15	0	10	522	370
1973-1974	25	15	2	8	435	294
1974-1975	16	5	0	11	207	244
1975-1976	25	14	1	10	438	342
1976-1977	20	12	0	8	348	269
1977-1978	23	14	0	9	322	301
1978-1979	18	12	0	6	246	203
1979-1980	22	13	2	7	257	222
1980-1981	27	15	2	10	401	335
1981-1982	20	13	4	3	325	176

	PLAYED	WON	DREW	LOST	POINTS FOR	POINTS AGAINST
1982-1983	27	5	2	20	283	446
1983-1984	19	11	0	8	378	285
1984-1985	20	9	0	11	341	262
1985-1986	24	14	0	10	449	333
1986-1987	23	13	0	10	411	317
1987-1988	20	9	3	8	265	293
1988-1989	23	14	1	8	421	318
1989-1990	19	12	1	6	338	295
1990-1991	16	9	0	7	397	184
1991-1992	19	12	1	6	338	242
1992-1993	20	12	0	8	405	259
1993-1994	18	6	1	11	275	339
1994-1995	17	9	1	7	364	359
1995-1996	18	6	1	11	390	369
1996-1997	19	8	0	11	384	626
1997-1998	23	8	1	14	523	646
1998-1999	16	3	0	13	259	390
1999-2000	15	7	1	7	414	393
2000-2001	18	6	0	12	354	498
2001-2002	19	10	0	9	529	439
2002-2003	17	9	2	6	443	401
2003-2004	15	6	0	9	281	363
2004-2005	16	6	1	9	281	363
2005-2006	17	9	1	7	434	275
2006-2007	16	5	2	9	322	389
2007-2008	17	8	0	9	400	344
2008-2009	33	19	0	14	680	656

AWAY – RECORD

The record for away victories is shared in the seasons of 1971-72, 1972-73, 1973-74, 1980-81. In 1971-72 when Mike Nicholls was the Club Captain we recorded 15 victories from 26 matches played in away fixtures. They were at Broughton Park 24-9, Bath 12-3, Bedford 13-3, Cheltenham 18-6, Pontypool 29-0, Cambridge University 13-6, Bristol 15-4, Bridgend 6-0, Bath 28-7, London Welsh 9-4, Newport 9-3, Lydney 16-6, Sale 12-3, Penzance 21-13 and Moseley 17-6. One match was drawn at Coventry 6-6.

The following season of 1972-73 there was a repeat act of 15 victories with John Bayliss as the Club Captain. The 15 wins from 25 away fixtures came from the following matches: Ebbw Vale 22-14, Stroud 35-10, Harlequins 13-0, South Wales Police 19-4, Aberavon 27-10, Oxford University 9-8, Wasps 22-11, Pontypool 13-6, Newbridge 23-18, Clifton 39-4, Cheltenham 39-4, Exeter 18-15, Lydney 32-12, Penzance & Newlyn 48-19, Camborne 70-9. Mike Nicholl's team of 1973-74 again repeated the feat of 15 away wins at Stroud 28-9, Moseley 24-4, Cheltenham 13-0, Clifton 34-3 Leicester 29-6, Combined Universities 16-10, Newbridge 21-0, London Scottish 21-0, Guy's Hospital 29-3, Bath 19-15, Lydney 15-6, Sale 18-3, Plymouth Albion 7-3, Penzance and Newlyn 21-13, Camborne 19-13.

It was eight season's later when Steve Mills was the Club Captain that the record of 15 away wins was equalled again in the season of 1980-81. Those victories came from these fixtures: Stroud 31-6, Ebbw Vale 18-10, Cheltenham 20-6, Pontypool 17-15, Nottingham 22-15, Plymouth Albion 26-6, Oxford University 27-3, Bath 19-0, Moseley 16-6, Bristol 7-0, London Irish 22-13, Saracens 12-11, Camborne 28-7, Lydney 23-13, Southend 12-6. There were two away matches that were drawn at London Scottish 9-9, and Headingly 6-6

AVERAGE

Since the innovation of the play-off system in the season of 2002-03 the four leading clubs in the Premier League have recorded the following points in the normal league season. Albeit that initially only the top three participated in the play-offs in the first season.

2002-03	Gloucester 82	2003-04	Bath 79
	London Wasps 67		London Wasps 73
	Northampton Saints 62		Sale Sharks 60
	Sale Sharks 62		Bath 58
2005-06	Sale Sharks 74	2006-07	Gloucester 71
	Leicester Tigers 71		Leicester Tigers 71
	London Irish 66		Bristol 64
	London Wasps 64		Saracens 63
2007-08	Gloucester 74	2008-09	Leicester 71
	London Wasps 70		Harlequins 66
	Bath 69		London Irish 66
	Leicester Tigers 64		Bath 65

AGGREGATES – ACCUMULATED

Since the game of Rugby Union turned professional in 1996 it is interesting to see which clubs the 'Cherry and Whites', have scored the most points against and to whom they have conceded.

Dealing with League matches played at Kingsholm these are the total of points we have accumulated against each club. In alphabetical order they are:

	HOME		AWAY	
TEAM	POINTS	MATCHES	POINTS	MATCHES
Bath	327	13	190	13
Bedford	91	2	33	2
Bristol	334	10	261	10
Harlequins	292	12	232	12
Leeds	195	6	191	6
Leicester	307	13	240	13
London Irish	339	13	244	13
London Scottish	29	1	13	1
Newcastle	366	12	227	12
Northampton	280	12	196	11
Orrell	30	1	49	1
Richmond	50	2	47	2
Rotherham	72	2	64	2
Sale	387	13	271	13
Saracens	337	13	274	13
Wasps	307	13	207	12
West Hartlepool	73	2	55	2
Worcester	117	4	80	4

All statistics upto and including 4th May 2009.

AGGREGATES – CONCEDED

These are the total of points we have conceded at Kingsholm against each club in League fixtures:

	HOME		AWAY	
TEAM	POINTS	MATCHES	POINTS	MATCHES
Bath	261	13	391	13
Bedford	38	2	25	2
Bristol	150	10	197	10
Harlequins	254	12	318	12
Leeds	102	6	116	6
Leicester	261	13	329	13
London Irish	191	13	323	13
London Scottish	13	1	24	1
Newcastle	248	12	279	12
Northampton	227	12	250	11
Orrell	0	1	3	1
Richmond	44	2	55	2
Rotherham	25	2	49	2
Sale	221	13	338	13
Saracens	181	13	357	13
Wasps	279	13	330	12
West Hartlepool	13	2	47	2
Worcester	58	4	69	4

All statistics upto and including 4th May 2009.

B

J. F. BROWN

J. F. Brown served as Captain for more consecutive seasons than any other player in the Club's history. His tenure lasted from 1876-1882.

BEHOLD – 'B'

W. A. Boughton, Tom Bagwell, Harold Boughton, Mickey Booth, John Bayliss, C. E. Brown, Mike Burton, Peter Buxton and Marco Bortolami have all been appointed as Club Captain.

B's TO BEAT

Barbarians, Bath, Bristol, Bective Rangers, Bedford, Begles, Bennetton-Treviso, Beziers, Biarritz, Birkenhead, Birkenhead Park, Blackheath, Bradford, Bream, Bridgend, Bridgwater, Broughton, Broughton Park, Broughton Rangers, British Police, Brixham, Bourgoin, Bosuns, Bucharest, Burton-On-Trent, Bayonne, Brive and Bristol Medicals.

BURTON-ON-TRENT

Burton-on-Trent provided the first opposition when the Club moved from the Spa to Kingsholm on 10th October 1891. The teams lined up as follows:

Gloucester:
A. F. Hughes; T. Bagwell (Captain), W. Jackson, T. B. Powell, W. H. Taylor; N. George, S. A. Ball; H. V. Page, A. Cromwell, A. E. Healing, C. Williams, A. Collins, T. Williams, A. Henshaw and H. Browne.

Burton-on-Trent:

T. P. Ward; G. A. Marsden, W. S. Lowe, F. M. Sadler, F. Evershed; T. C. Gorton, E. Evershed; T. Clitheroe, H. Mauger, W. N. Greenwell, A. Gorton, H. C. Gorton, F. Lloyd, T. Robinson and H. Browne.

BATH AND BRISTOL

Bath and Bristol are famed opponents from the West Country. Matches where pride and passion are at stake. The first match played versus Bath at Kingsholm was played in the 1895-96 season and resulted in a pointless encounter 0-0! The away encounter in the same season also resulted in a drawn match, although this time there were points registered in a 3-3 result. Bristol travelled to Kingsholm in the 1892-93 season for the first time. A 14 points to nil defeat was inflicted by the 'Cherry and Whites'. The return fixture in that same season resulted in a drawn match 2-2.

BLAKEWAY AND BURTON

Two of the most outstanding prop forwards to have played for the 'Cherry and Whites' have been Phil Blakeway and Mike Burton.

MIKE BURTON

Mike Burton was born on 18th December 1945 in Maidenhead, Berkshire. He is widely regarded as one of the most colourful characters to have played for Gloucester Rugby and England.

He was actually christened Michael Alan Harrop, using his mother's name until she married Denis Burton of Gloucester. Mike, was educated at Longlevens School in the City of Gloucester.

He represented both Berkshire and Gloucestershire in the County Championship. Mike was capped on 17 occasions by England and made his debut versus Wales at Twickenham on 15th January 1972 in the following XV.

R. Hillier (Harlequins) Captain; J. P. A. J. Jannion (Bedford), M. C. Beese (Liverpool), D. J. Duckham (Coventry), K. J. Fielding (Moseley); A. G. B. Old (Middlesborough), J. G. Webster (Moseley); C. B. Stevens (Harlequins), J. V. Pullin (Bristol), M. A. H. Burton (Gloucester), A. Brinn (Gloucester), C. W. Ralston (Richmond), P. J. Dixon (Harlequins), A. G. Ripley (Rosslyn Park) and A. Neary (Broughton Park).

The prop forward had the unenviable record of having been sent off in both hemispheres of the rugby world! Playing for England versus Australia in 1975, thus becoming the first Englishman to be dismissed in an International match and in the same year playing for Gloucestershire against Hertfordshire.

Mike made 360 appearances for Gloucester Rugby appearing in two Knock Out Cup Finals in 1972 versus Moseley and in 1978 versus Leicester, both matches played at Twickenham.

PHIL BLAKEWAY

The former England prop forward made 19 appearances for his country. Phil joined Gloucester Rugby in 1972. In a match versus South Wales Police in 1978 he suffered a broken neck. He was a member of England's 1980 Grand Slam team against France that year when he suffered a broken rib.

Phil retired from the game in 1981 and again in 1982 but changed his mind and amazingly each time regained his England place. A former British Under-21 modern pentathlon champion in 1968 and he was also reserve that year for the world junior championships.

A former Barbarian and British Lion tourist he made his debut for England versus Ireland on 19th January 1980 in the following XV:

W. H. Hare (Leicester); J. Carleton (Orrell), A. M. Bond (Sale), N. J. Preston (Richmond), M. A. C. Slemen (Liverpool); J. P. Horton (Bath), S. J. Smith (Sale); F. E. Cotton (Sale), P. J. Wheeler (Leicester), P. J. Blakeway (Gloucester), W. B. Beaumont (Fylde) Captain, N. E. Horton (Moseley), R. M. Uttley (Wasps), J. P. Scott (Cardiff) and A. Neary (Broughton Park).

Phil captained the South and South West Divisional team on three occasions against overseas touring teams – Australia in 1981, Fiji in 1982 and New Zealand in 1983. He was a member of the Gloucester Rugby team that shared the National Cup with Moseley in 1982 following a 12 points apiece tie. His final comeback from retirement saw Phil play for Moseley at the age of 41.

ALAN BRINN

Lock forward capped twice for England although he was actually born in Ystrad, Rhonnda, Wales. Alan joined the Club in 1962 and when his playing retirement came in 1977 he had made an astonishing 572 appearances for the 'Cherry and Whites'. This is a record unlikely to be surpassed due to the reduced fixture list compared with the seasons when Alan played.

Following his retirement he became an England Rugby Union associate national selector. Alan also served the Club in the official capacity as Chairman.

BEST OF THE 'B's

Capped by England at International Level:

Scott Benton, Henry Berry, Phil Blakeway, Harold Boughton, Steve Boyle, Alan Brinn, Alex Brown, Mike Burton and Peter Butler.

NATIONAL CUP WINNERS – B

Steve Baker	1982
John Bayliss	1972
Micky Booth	1972
Alan Brinn	1972
Mike Burton	1972 and 1978
Peter Butler	1978
Steve Boyle	1978 and 1982
Phil Blakeway	1982
Jake Boer	2003

BUTLER THE BOOT

Peter Butler accumulated 2,961 points scored between 1972 and 1982.

BOOTH THE BEST

During his career at Kingsholm the much-admired scrum half, Mickey Booth set a club record with 41 dropped goals.

BOOTH AND BAYLISS

Mickey Booth and John Bayliss both made over 400 appearances for the 'Cherry and Whites'.

BOUNTY

Fullback Harold Boughton recorded 1,240 points for the Club.

BROTHERS

The only brothers to have played for England from Gloucester Rugby Club were Frank and Percy Stout who appeared in the International matches versus Wales and Scotland in 1898.

BOOKS

Three books have been written by or on behalf of former Gloucester Rugby Football Club players:

Rubbing Shoulders by Phil Blakeway.
Never Stay Down by Mike Burton.
Rugby Football by Dai Gent.

BUTLER 'THE BOOT'

Peter Butler holds the Gloucester R.F.C. record for conversions in a season. In the 1960-61 campaign he kicked a total of 61.

BOOTING AGAIN

Peter Butler also holds the Gloucester R.F.C. record for penalties in a season. In the 1973-74 season he kicked a total of 114.

BAN FROM THE LOCAL COUNCIL

A ban was placed upon the Club, then known as Gloucester Football Club in 1879 from playing at The Spa. The City Council banned rugby from the park due to damage to shrubbery following a match in January of that year. Stating bad behaviour eminated from the dangerously large crowd of 2,000.

BAN LIFTED

In September 1879 the ban was defeated following a deputation from local football clubs and the Headmaster of Crypt School who collected over 2,500 signatures.

BATH THE FIRST

It is believed that the first match played at the Spa with South-West rivals Bath took place on 2nd December 1882 and resulted in a 12 points to nil victory. Try scorers were H. Coates, Sloman and Dewey. Goals were kicked by Boughton, Jones and Berry.

A BATH NEXT DOOR

The earliest matches played against Bath in away fixtures were staged at Lambridge. Other matches played within the confines of the City of Bath have been played at Henrietta Park owned by Bath College.

MR BAGWELL

A 'working man' was elected to Captain the Club in 1890. He was Tommy Bagwell who was a labourer at the local Wagon Works. This was the press description of the former Club Captain. Tommy, was the first Captain when the Club commenced playing at Kingsholm.

BORN

'Born and bred' was the proud boast in 1898 when every player with the Club came from the locality.

BASS

Bass sponsored Gloucester Rugby Football Club in 1989. A sponsorship that lasted to the end of the 1993/94 season.

GONE FOR A BURTON

Mike Burton (Sports Management) Ltd was engaged by the Club in 1990 to undertake all the commercial, sales, hospitality and sponsorship activities.

BROWN THE FIRST

Hamish Brown was appointed as an Executive Director of the Club in 1998 joining from Tom Walkinshaw Racing.

A BRISTOL DAY IN FOG

The only International staged at Ashton Gate, the home of Bristol City Football Club, saw England lose by 28 points to eighteen. On a foggy damp day the players repeatedly disappeared from sight. Included in the England team were Arthur Hudson and Arthur Wood from Gloucester Rugby Football Club. That match was staged on 18th January 1908.

BOUGHTON THE SAVIOUR

Harold Boughton of Gloucester Rugby Football Club saved England in 1935 from the Wooden Spoon with his kicking ability. His penalty tied the match with Wales on 19th January and his four successful goal kicks against Ireland on 9th February proved the difference between the teams. Both matches were played at Twickenham. Only one try was scored by an England three quarter during that season, the worst return since 1905.

'SACRE BLEU'

Phil Blakeway was a member of the England team that lost to France on 21st March 1981. Yet it was a defeat to a try which should not have been awarded. The French scored from a quick throw in but the law prescribes that only the ball that went into touch may be retrieved by the players for the throw. The French took their opportunity with a ball supplied by a bystander. France won by 16 points to twelve.

BEATEN

Scott Benton, former Gloucester Rugby Club scrum half appeared for England in their heaviest reverse ever. Scott, who was making his debut in his one and only International appearance was accompanied by his club colleague Phil Vickery in a 76 points to nil reverse versus Australia on 6th June 1988.

BATHED AND BEATEN

Bath R.F.C. fielded a full 15-man team of Internationals against Gloucester R.F.C. on 26 September 1998. This was the first time this had occurred in a Premiership match. Played at the Recreation Ground, Bath the hosts were victors by 21 points to 16.

BALSHAW

Iain Balshaw has scored 12 tries for England and lies in 14th position in the full list of players who have scored ten or more tries for England.

ALL THE B's

Following the Second World War 1939-45 the first visitors to Kingsholm were Bristol. Gloucester captained by Harold Boughton won convincingly by eighteen points to nil.

WHAT A BOON

In 1905, C. Boon, a Gloucester supporter, completed the XV to face Cardiff at the Arms Park in 1905 having been selected from the crowd attending the match. It was the only match in which he played! Two Gloucester players had missed the train!

BACK AGAIN

Iain Balshaw, the Gloucester utility back had been recalled a record 9 times by England when the 2008 Six Nations Championship were staged.

BARBARIANS

In that one and only fixture with Gloucester R.F.C. the Barbarians appeared at Kingsholm on 26th March 1891. Gloucester defeated the Ba-Baa's by 10 points to nine.

BUCKINGHAM PALACE

The three heroes of England's World Cup success in Australia 2003 were invited to Buckingham Palace to meet Queen Elizabeth II – they were Andy Gomarsall, Phil Vickery and Trevor Woodman, all Gloucester Rugby Club players.

OLLY BARKLEY

Olly, the Club's 2008 signing from West Country rivals Bath actually played for a New Zealand club – Marist. The Hammersmith born, Colston School educated back actually made his International debut for England in San Francisco! Olly was the 1,531st player to be capped by his country.

HENRY BERRY

Former Gloucester prop forward, Henry Berry, was killed in action in Festeburt in France in 1915 during the First World War. Educated at St Marks School in the City he was the 492nd player to be capped by England. Henry scored a try in his last appearance for his country at Inverleith versus Scotland on 19th March 1910. Henry made four appearances for England. For Gloucester Rugby Club he made 137 appearances scoring 27 tries. Henry, was one of 27 England Internationals who forfeited their lives in the First World War. He had previously been awarded the Queen's Medal during the South Africa conflict.

ALL THREE FOR BROWN

Alex Brown, the Gloucester Rugby Club lock forward has belonged to all three West Country Clubs, Bath, Bristol and Gloucester. The Colston's School educated lock has also played for Pontypool. Alex was the 1,269th player to represent England when he made his International debut in Sydney on 11th June 2006 versus Australia.

BAKER

There have been five players with the surname of Baker that have appeared at 1st XV level: C. Baker, J. Baker, J. M. Baker, M. Baker and R. L. Baker.

BROWN

There have been nine players with the surname of Brown who have played for Gloucester: A. Brown 1902, Alex Brown 2003, C. E. Brown 1891, D. J. Brown 1919-1921, F. Brown 1921-1923, H. G. Brown 1891-1892, P. Brown 1938-1939 and S. Brown 1919-1925 and Alex Brown 2003-?.

'BOOTIFUL BUTLER'

Gloucester full back Peter Butler with his final kick of the 1973/74 season enabled him to set a new world record at club level. It allowed him to become the first man player to score over 1,000 points in two years.

STEVE BOYLE

Former Gloucester and England lock forward Steve Boyle who joined the Club from Old Richians actually made his debut for the Club in the front row against London Irish on 24th November 1973; he played alongside Mike Nicholls and Keith Richardson. Along with John Dix and Phil Winnel, Steve was one of three players who had not appeared in the County Championship in the Club's line-up that day. The other twelve players had all represented Gloucestershire.

BOYLE LATER

Steve Boyle in his years of retirement from playing has acted as Team Manager for the England Veterans XV who have participated in the Bahamas Classic Veterans competition.

BROWN SETS A RECORD

Gloucester Rugby Football Club lock forward Alex Brown set a Premiership record of 88 consecutive appearances in October 2005 when overtaking Derek Eves total of 87 for Bristol.

BARBARIANS

There have been many Gloucester R.F.C. players who have represented the Barbarians either when they were on the Kingsholm playing staff or before joining or leaving the Club.

Among those who have been honoured by this exclusive Club are Phil Blakeway, Steve Boyle, Mike Burton, Scott Benton, Warren Bullock, Alf Carpenter, Nathan Carter, Andy Deacon, Peter Ford, Chris Fortey, Andy Gomarsall, George Hastings, Peter Hordern, Richard Hill, David Lougheed, Ian Jones, Maurice McCanlis, Steve Ojomoh, Dean Ryan, Don Rutherford, David Sims, Philippe St Andre, Frank Stout, Percy Stout, Ian Smith, Mike Teague, Paul Turner, Richard West and Tom Voyce.

JAKE BOER

South African born Jake Boer took the Zurich Player of the Season in 2002/2003 and ended the season with nine tries, the best by a forward in the Zurich Premiership.

BEASTLY BARKLEY

In the season of 2006-2007 two players moved into joint 12th position on the all times list of scoring the most penalties in a match Olly did so with 7 when he kicked those versus Gloucester on 7th April 2007. The record is held jointly by Thierry Lacroix (Saracens) and Simon Mannix who both recorded 9 in a single match. Simon did so on 23rd September 2000 versus Harlequins at Kingsholm.

BROWN AND BAYLISS

Sid Brown who met an untimely injury resulting in his death, made his debut for Gloucester against Abertillery in September 1919. He scored two tries in this match. As a schoolboy he played for England and represented both Gloucestershire and Lancashire. He was also a 100 yard sprinter for Gloucester Amateur Athletic Club where his father was the Chairman.

Both Sid Brown and Stan Bayliss who also died of injury sustained at Kingsholm are buried in Gloucester Cemetery. Both graves are at the rear of the Cross of Sacrifice:

Sid Brown   –   after his 182nd appearance versus Aberavon in 1926.
Stan Bayliss –   after his 100th appearance versus Old Blues in 1925.

OLLY BARKLEY

Olly Barkley, the Club's 2008 summer signing from West County rivals Bath, first attracted attention when he played in two successive Daily Mail Under 18 Schools cup-winning teams while at Colston's Collegiate, Bristol and captained the team in 2000.

BASKETBALL!

Olly Barkley had trials for Plymouth Argyle Football Club; he was offered another trial with Arsenal but at the time preferred basketball! It was a shrewd P.E. teacher at Wadebridge School who insisted he had to play rugby as well if he wanted to play football.

THE BOSUNS

When the long awaited match to celebrate the 'christening' of the floodlights at Kingsholm on 6th November 1967, The Bosuns team that faced Gloucester R.F.C. on that Monday evening was:

B. B. Wright (Brighton); P. C. Sibley (Bath), P. J. Burnett (London Scottish), D. J. J. Allanson (Rosslyn Park), M. R. Collins (Bristol); T. D. Wright (St Luke's College), D. T. Stevens (Blackheath); A. L. Horton (Blackheath), I. A. Hart (New Brighton), D. L. Powell (Northampton), P. A. Eastwood (United Services, Portsmouth), D. E. J. Watts (Bristol), P. J. Bell (Blackheath), J. Barton (Coventry) and D. Phillips (St Luke's College and Bristol).

David Powell is now the Groundsman at Franklins Gardens, home of Northampton Saints.

BONUS POINTS

They were introduced for the 2000-2001 season. Four points are awarded for scoring 4 or more tries, and a single point if losing by seven points or less. Here is the Club's record since that innovation season by season.

FOUR TRIES		
	HOME	AWAY
2000-01	Versus Bristol won 38-16 (Little 2, Azam, Vickery)	Versus Rotherham won 29-23 (Schisano 3, Jewell)
2001-02	Versus Rotheham won 50-17 (Beim, Catling, Cornwell, Todd, Simpson-Daniel, Little, Penalty Try)	
	Versus Bristol won 51-17 (Gomarsall, Paramore, Catling, Fortey, Hazell, Simpson-Daniel)	Versus Sale won 44-21 (Woodman, Yachvili, Pucciariello, Fanolua)
	Versus Leeds won 58-17 (Simpson-Daniel 2, O'Leary, Paul. Garvey, Todd, Eustace)	Versus Bristol won 41-40 (Paramore 2, Gomarsall, Sewabu, Vickery)
	Versus Sale won 42-14 (Paramore, Pucciariello, Gomarsall, Simpson-Daniel, Forrester)	Versus Leeds won 50-17 (Simpson-Daniel 2, O'Leary Paramore, Sewabu, Woodman, Forrester)
	Versus Wasps Won 43-13 (Azam 2, Boer, Penalty Try)	
	Versus Bath Won 68-12 (Fanolua 2, Simpson-Daniel 3, Paul, Paramore, Todd, Vickery)	
2002-03	Versus Sale won 44-8 (Forrester 2, Boer, Paul, Beim, Delport)	Versus Bristol won 38-21 (Forrester 3, Hazell, Mercier, Garvey)
	Versus Bristol won 44-14 (Garvey 3, Paramore, Boer, Mercier)	
	Versus Saracens won 45-18 (Azam 2, Fanolua, Boer, Mercier)	
	Versus London Irish Won 40-19 (Eustace, Paramore, Forrester, Boer, Roncero)	
	Versus Harlequins Won 29-11 (Mercier, Simpson-Daniel, Boer, Paul)	
2003-04	Versus Saracens won 30-7 (Goodridge 2, Simpson-Daniel, Forrester)	
	Versus Newcastle won 36-12 (Forrester, Garvey, Todd, McRae, Fanolua)	

	Versus Sale won 38-12 (Roncero 2, Paramore, Boer)	
	Versus Rotherham won 35-12 (Forrester 2, Fanolua 2)	
2004-05	Versus Sale won 24-14 (Goodridge, Garvey, Fanolua, Fortey)	Versus Newcastle Drew 27-27 (Garvey, Fanolua, Gomarsall, Narraway)
	Versus Harlequins Won 29-23 (Fanolua 2, Paul, Simpson-Daniel)	
2005-06	Versus Leeds won 31-7 (Simpson-Daniel 2, Mercier, Penalty Try)	Versus Leeds won 31-7 (Tindall, Simpson-Daniel, Richards, Hazell)
	Versus Wasps lost 32-37 (Allen 2, Lamb, Bailey)	Versus Bristol won 41-9 (Forrester 2, Thomas, Goodridge)
2006-07	Versus Sale won 44-24 (Morgan, Balshaw, Lamb, Azam, Bortolami)	
	Versus Harlequins won 34-25 (Foster, Bailey, Wood, Forrester)	
	Versus Bristol won 35-13 (Ashton Gate) (Foster, Walker, Hazell, Boer)	
2007-08	Versus Leeds won 49-24 (Vainikolos 5, Allen, Simpson-Daniel, Balshaw) Versus Bristol won 27-0 (Simpson-Daniel, Azam, Lloyd 2)	Versus Harlequins lost 25-30 (Simpson-Daniel 2, Allen, Adams)
	Versus London Irish won 34-14 (Adams, Wood, Foster, Titterell)	
	Versus Saracens Won 39-15 (Lamb 2, Vainikolo, Lawson, Qera, Simpson-Daniel)	
	Versus Leeds won 39-16 (Qera 3, Lamb, Azam)	
2008-09	Versus Newcastle Won 39-23 (Balshaw 3, Simpson-Daniel 2)	Versus Bristol Won 29-10 (Tindall 2, Vainikolo, Morgan)
	Versus Bristol won 39-10 (Buxton 2, Morgan, Brown, Lamb)	
	Versus Northampton won 33-10 (Balshaw, Narraway, Barkley, Vainikolo)	
	Versus Bath won 36-27 Simpson-Daniel 2, Charples, Lawson	

BONUS POINTS – WITHIN 7 POINTS		
	HOME	AWAY
2000-01	Sale (lost) 18-19 Bath (lost) 21-22 Northampton (lost) 12-15	Leicester (lost) 28-31 Harlequins (lost) 19-21
2001-02		Saracens (lost) 30-34 London Irish (lost) 15-19 Newcastle (lost) 16-18 Bath (lost) 9-12
2002-03		Wasps (lost) 16-23 Leicester (lost) 15-20 Leeds (lost) 25-30
2003-04	Bath (lost) 14-20	London Irish (lost) 10-16 Leeds (lost) 18-22
2004-05	Saracens (lost) 13-14	Saracens (lost) 9-14
2005-06	Bristol (lost) 15-20 London Irish (lost) 9-13 Bath (lost) 15-18 Wasps (lost) 32-37	Bath (lost) 16-18 Leicester (lost) 20-25 Wasps (lost) 25-32 Northampton (lost) 20-21 Sale (lost) 15-18
2006-07		Bristol (lost) 12-14 Sale (lost) 19-20 Saracens (lost) 22-24 Newcastle (lost) 12-19
2007-08		London Irish (lost) 10-15 Bath (lost) 5-10 Bristol (lost) 26-29 Harlequins (lost) 25-30 Sale (lost) 16-22 Worcester (lost) 14-17
2008-09		Newcastle (lost) 7-10 Harlequins (lost) 9-14

BATH

The 'Cherry and Whites', rivalry with the West Country rivals is renowned throughout English rugby. It is interesting to look at the results home and away since the clubs first met, obviously in an amateur era until the advent of professional rugby in 1996. These are the results since the birth of Kingsholm.

SEASON	HOME		AWAY	
1895-96	Drew	0-0	Drew	3-3
1896-97	Won	27-0	Won	14-0
1897-98	Won	11-0	Won	11-0
1898-99	Won	8-0	Won	18-0
1899-00	Won	21-0	Won	20-0
1900-01	Won	33-0	Won	10-0
1901-02	Won	21-3	Won	26-0
1902-03	–	–	Won	26-0
1903-04	Won	25-0	Drew	8-8
1904-05	Won	8-5	Won	11-6
1905-06	Won	16-0	Won	3-0

1906/1907 – 1912/1913   NO GAMES

1913-14	Won	19-0	Won	10-3
1919-20	Won	16-6	Won	24-0
1920-21	Won	9-6	Won	8-0
1921-22	Drew	9-9	Won	13-3
1922-23	Won	17-5	Lost	6-9
1923-24	Won	18-8	Lost	5-12
1924-25	Won	21-0	Lost	7-16
1925-26	Won	17-3	Lost	0-3
1926-27	Won	13-6	Won	6-5
1927-28	Won	8-5	Lost	8-10
1928-29	Won	6-0	–	–
1929-30	Won	3-3	Drew	3-3
1930-31	Won	13-0	Lost	3-9
1931-32	Won	8-3	Lost	3-8
1932-33	Won	17-3	Lost	0-3
1933-34	Won	23-8	Lost	8-13
1934-35	Won	17-0	Lost	0-3
1935-36	Won	6-3	Drew	3-3
1936-37	Won	7-3	Lost	5-11
1937-38	Won	10-0	Lost	0-3
1938-39	Lost	3-5	Lost	5-6
1939-40	Drew	3-3	–	–
1945-46	Lost	11-13	Won	27-8
1946-47	Won	27-9	Lost	3-8
1947-48	Won	15-0	Won	14-8
1948-49	Won	5-0	Lost	3-13
1949-50	Won	3-0	Lost	11-14

SEASON	HOME		AWAY	
1950-51	Won	27-3	Lost	3-8
1951-52	–	–	Lost	0-3
1952-53	Won	11-3	Lost	0-11
1953-54	Won	14-5	Won	9-6
1954-55	Won	11-3	Won	21-0
1955-56	–	–	Won	11-0
1956-57	Won	27-6	Lost	0-11
1957-58	Won	15-3	Won	9-6
1958-59	Drew	8-8	Drew	3-3
1959-60	Won	9-3	Won	12-3
1960-61	Won	17-8	Won	8-3
1961-62	Won	9-3	Drew	8-8
1962-63	Won	19-3	–	-
1963-64	Won	14-0	Won	19-11
1964-65	Won	13-3	Won	8-6
1965-66	Won	12-9	Lost	13-19
1966-67	Lost	9-14	Won	16-11
1967-68	Lost	6-18	Won	11-0
1968-69	Won	8-6	Won	19-13
1969-70	Won	39-13	–	–
1970-71	Drew	9-9		0-0
1971-72	Won	24-16	RFU National Cup	12-3
	–	–	Won	28-7
1972-73 RFU National Cup	Won	16-0	–	–
	Won	18-16	Lost	7-16
1973-74	Won	18-8	Won	19-15
1974-75	Won	28-3	Lost	7-12
1975-76	Won	12-3	Won	18-15
1976-77	Won	51-7	-	-
1977-78	Won	24-13	Won	12-10
1978-79	Won	11-3	Lost	10-20
1979-80	Won	10-3	Lost	9-24
1980-81	Won	15-10	Won	19-0
1981-82	Won	33-15	Won	12-6
1982-83	Drew	7-7	Lost	12-21
1983-84	Won	16-8	Lost	6-13
1984-85	–	–	Lost	9-19
			Lost RFU National Cup	11-12

SEASON	HOME		AWAY	
1985-86				
League	Won	15-11	Lost	9-22
1986-87	–	–	Won	12-9
1987-88				
League	Lost	9-16	Drew	26-26
1988-89				
RFU				
National Cup	Lost	3-6	Lost	9-19
1989-90	Won	13-6	Lost	6-48
League			RFU National Cup	
1990-91	Lost	15-17	Lost	19-32
League				
1991-92	Won	14-12	Lost	9-29
R.F.U				
National Cup	Lost	18-27	–	–
1992-93				
League	Lost	0-20	Won	17-16
1993-94				
League	Lost	6-16	Lost	17-46
1994-95				
League	Lost	10-15	Drew	19-19
1995-96	Won	16-10	Lost	
			RFU National Cup	10-19
			Lost	11-37
1996-97				
League	Lost	29-45	Lost	21-71

SEASON	HOME		AWAY	
1997-98				
League	Won	27-17	Lost	3-47
1998-99				
League	Won	23-7	Lost	16-21
1999-00				
RFU National				
Cup	Won	13-6	Lost	20-33
	Lost	16-36	–	–
2000-01				
League	Lost	21-22	Won	
			RFU National	
			Cup	24-18
			Lost	16-50
2001-02				
League	Won	68-12	Lost	9-12
2002-03				
League	Won	29-16	Drew	21-21
2003-04				
League	Lost	14-20	Lost	7-41
2004-05				
League	Won	17-16	Lost	14-29
2005-06				
League	Lost	15-18	Lost	16-18
2006-07				
League	Won	24-19	Drew	21-21
2008-09				
League	Won	36-27	Won	21-17

Fixtures were aborted from 1905-06 until 1913-14 due to the fact that Bath had been of insufficient strength to have won any of the 22 matches played.

BRILLIANT BALSHAW

When former Cherry and White utility back, Iain Balshaw, scored a try against London Irish at Kingsholm on 31st January 2009 he recorded the 50th try of his career. A career spent playing with Bath R.F.C., Leeds R.F.C. and Gloucester Rugby. Those fifty tries came as follows:

Bath R.F.C.:

Season 1997-98	Opposition	Venue	Date	Result	Tries
	Richmond	Away	13th April	Lost 14-32	1

	Opposition	Venue	Date	Result	Tries
	Bedford	Home	3rd October	Won 57-19	1
	London Irish	Home	10th October	Won 23-20	1
	West Hartlepool	Away	17th October	Won 50-20	1
	Harlequins	Away	21st November	Lost 31-43	1
Season 1998-99	Saracens	Home	19th December	Lost 11-19	1
	Bedford	Away	23rd January	Won 30-17	1
	Saracens	Away	28th March	Won 33-14	3
	Leicester	Home	3rd April	Won 24-16	1
	West Hartlepool	Home	24th April	Won 56-24	2
	London Scottish	Home	15th May	Won 76-13	1

	Opposition	Venue	Date	Result	Tries
	Northampton	Home	25th September	Won 33-13	1
	Bristol	Away	16th October	Drew 31-31	1
	Newcastle	Home	13th November	Won 45-12	1
	Wasps	Home	22nd January	Won 27-16	2
Season 1999-2000	Newcastle	Away	25th January	Won 20-16	1
	London Irish	Away	11th March	Won 64-16	2
	Bristol	Home	25th March	Won 39-13	2
	Gloucester	Away	8th April	Won 36-16	1
	Northampton	Away	22nd April	Won 17-13	1
	Harlequins	Home	29th April	Won 77-19	2
	Saracens	Home	6th May	Won 40-27	1

	Opposition	Venue	Date	Result	Tries
Season 2000-01	Gloucester	Away	9th September	Won 22-21	1
	London Irish	Home	23rd December	Won 56-20	1
	Leicester	Home	26th December	Lost 16-17	1
	Saracens	Away	30th December	Won 31-11	1
	Northampton	Home	6th January	Won 36-13	1
	Gloucester	Home	24th February	Won 50-16	1

	Opposition	Venue	Date	Result	Tries
Season 2002-03	Newcastle	Home	10th May	Won 24-12	1

Leeds R.F.C.:

	Opposition	Venue	Date	Result	Tries
Season 2005-06	Wasps	Home	18th September	Lost 23-47	1
	Saracens	Home	7th April	Lost 13-17	1

Gloucester Rugby:

	Opposition	Venue	Date	Result	Tries
Season 2006-07	Worcester	Away	13th October	Won 33-25	1
	London Irish	Home	1st January	Won 15-3	1
	Sale	Home	27th January	Won 44-24	1

	Opposition	Venue	Date	Result	Tries
Season 2007-08	Leeds	Away	16th September	Won 49-24	1
	London Irish	Away	21st October	Lost 10-15	1
	Newcastle	Away	23rd December	Won 20-13	1
	Harlequins	Away	1st March	Won 25-30	1

	Opposition	Venue	Date	Result	Tries
Season 2008-09	Newcastle	Home	30th September	Won 39-23	3
	Northampton	Home	29th November	Won 33-10	1
	London Irish	Home	31st January	Won 23-21	1
	Leicester	Away	7th March	Lost 10-24	1
	Wasps	Home	14th March	Won 24-22	1

The only clubs that Iain has failed to score a try against since the advent of professional rugby union are his former club Bath, and Orrell. Iain has scored 29 tries in home matches and 22 in away fixtures.

C

COLOURS

Gloucester Rugby Club have always played in the colours of 'Cherry and White', well at least for most of the Club's history. The traditionalists have always favoured the hoop design of the shirt. Commercial interest has dictated that in recent seasons a policy change has been adopted in colour and design.

CHANGING NAMES

Since the birth of the Club in 1873 it has been referred to in various guises varying from 'City' in 1901, to 'Citizens' by 1910, and 'Cherry and Whites' by 1957.

A CARPENTER HAPPY TO BE A JOINER

Alfred 'Bumps' Carpenter only made one appearance for England. 'Bumps' was born in Mitcheldean in the Forest of Dean on 23rd July 1900 and it was often reported that such was his enthusiasm to play for Gloucester Rugby Club that he would walk from his home in Cinderford to play!

His solitary cap for England came on 2nd January 1932 versus South Africa at Twickenham when no fewer than nine players were making their debut for England.

CHELTENHAM & GLOUCESTER CUP

The 'Cherry and Whites' defeated Bedford in the inaugural final on Friday 10th April 1998 in a 33 points to 25 triumph.

One year later on 9th April 1999 they retained the Cup when once again they disposed of Bedford by 24 points to 9.

Both matches were staged at Franklin's Garden, the home of Northampton Saints.

NATIONAL CUP WINNERS – C

Bob Clewes   1972 and 1978
Robin Cowling   1972

CLUBHOUSE

Erected in 1965 at a cost of £15,000. It was demolished in the summer of 2007.

CIVIL DEFENCE

During the Second World War 1939-1945 the ground was utilised by the Civil Defence.

COMPENSATION

The Club received £800 in compensation for the use of the ground during that period.

CAR PARK

The Kingsholm car park was once a football field where City Albion played and also the City Thursday team.

CRIGHTON-MILLER

Was the first player from the Club to win an International Cap with Scotland in 1931. Donald made 27 appearances for the Club scoring 4 tries.

COUNTY LEAGUE WINNERS

The Club were the winners of the Gloucestershire County League in the 1908-09 season.

COUNTY MATCH

The first County Match played at Kingsholm was on 17th December 1891 versus Devon.

CLERGYMAN

Christopher Champion Tanner was one of eighteen clergymen to have been capped by England.

CRICKET

Former Gloucester Rugby players to have played first class cricket:

Willie Jones, A. R. Lewis (Glamorgan), Graham Parker (Gloucestershire), Maurice McCanlis (Surrey), George Romans (Gloucestershire), Gilbert Jessop (Gloucestershire), H. J. Boughton (Gloucestershire), M. H. Cullimore (Gloucestershire) and H. V. Page (Gloucestershire).

CENTENARY YEAR

Centenary Year was celebrated in 1973.

CONVERTING TO A RECORD

The most conversions recorded in a career with Gloucester Rugby Football Club are the total of 424 by Harold Boughton who made 345 appearances for Gloucester R.F.C.

CAPTAIN – FIRST AT CLUB

The first Gloucester captain was Francis Hartley who was appointed from 1873 to 1875.

CHANGES

James Simpson-Daniel and Andy Gomarsall appeared on the only occasion that England has changed all fifteen players from those that had appeared in the previous match. They played for England on 23rd August 2003 at the Millennium Stadium, Cardiff versus Wales. In the previous International Phil Vickery and Trevor Woodman, both of Gloucester Rugby Club had appeared on 21st June 2003 versus Australia.

CROWDS

Crowds began to increase significantly in the 1880/81 season when attendances of 3 and 4000 paying spectators attended matches versus Clifton, Moseley and Newport. Matches were then played at the Spa.

THE CITIZEN

The first match reports appeared in *The Citizen* newspaper in the 1886/87 season. This was a season where ten of the first fifteen were born in the City and it was expounded that no outsiders were welcome!

CITIZEN SPORTS 'THE PINK UN'

The Citizen published its first Saturday sports edition in 1891.

CINEMAS

Cinemas in the City showed the Gloucester versus New Zealand match played on 10th October 1905. The match was recorded on 'cinematograph'.

CAPTAIN OF ENGLAND

Former Gloucester Rugby Club players who have Captained England are Phil Vickery and John Orwin. Phil captained England whilst at Kingsholm when he led England to a stirring 26-18 victory over Argentina in Buenos Aires on 22nd June 2002. John Orwin was appointed England Captain after joining Bedford. He led England to a 21-10 victory versus Ireland in Dublin on 3rd April 1988.

CROWD TROUBLE

Crowd disorder was prevalent when Bristol defeated the City in the final of the County Cup in 1907. The referee was mobbed, struck, kicked and needed police protection.

CELEBRATION

In 1952 the Club celebrated 60 years at Kingsholm with thirty victories in the 1951/52 season.

MR COLEY

Mike Coley was appointed as the Club's first Marketing Manager in 1985.

CORLESS THE FIRST

Barry Corless was appointed as the Club's first full-time paid Director of Rugby at a salary of £40,000 per annum in 1993 at the age of 47. He left in February 1995.

CHAIRMAN

The Club Chairman, Peter Ford, re-stated in 1994 the Club's traditional anti-professionalism position saying, 'We play by the rules, whatever anybody decides. We'll stick by the ruler. If they say we can't pay players or offer them inducements or cars or flats ... then we won't do it'.

CHIEF EXECUTIVE – CAST ADRIFT

In May 1996 the post of the Chief Executive was made redundant and Mike Coley therefore departed from Kingsholm.

COURAGE LEAGUE

Courage League One Clubs, including Gloucester were in a prolonged dispute in 1995 with the Rugby Football Union about control of the game and the commercial potential of television rights.

COLOURS

The earliest known colour photograph of a Gloucester team with captions was taken in 1897.

CAPTAINS IN 'DUAL'

The club had dual captains appointed for the 1946-47 season for the second time in their history – Tom Price and Roy Morris. In the 1904-05 season George Romans and Bill Johns had captained R.F.C. in a dual role.

THE ONLY 'C'

Alfred Carpenter is the only player with a surname commencing with the letter 'C' to have played for England from Gloucester Rugby Football Club.

ALL THE 'C's

OPPONENTS: Caerphilly, Cambridge University, Camborne, Captain Dunnes XV, Cardiff, Cardiff and District, Cardiff Harlequins, Carlisle, Canterbury (New Zealand), Casale, Cascais (Portugal), Castleford, Cheltenham, Cinderford, Civil Service, Clifton, Combined Services, Combined Universities, Colomiers, Coventry, Cross Keys and Colomier.

COUNTY CHAMPIONSHIP RECORD

Alfred 'Bumps' Carpenter had a remarkable County Championship record for Gloucestershire – 52 appearances, played in six semi-finals and five finals of which he was on the winning side on four occasions.

COURAGE THE FIRST

The first official league structure in English rugby was the Courage League in the 1987-88 season. The clubs in finishing order at the end of that season were as follows:

1. Leicester, 2. Wasps, 3. Harlequins, 4. Bath, 5. Gloucester R.F.C., 6. Orrell, 7. Moseley, 8. Nottingham, 9. Bristol, 10. Waterloo, 11. Coventry, 12. Sale.

CLUB COLOURS

The Club colours have been red and white since they borrowed a set of Cherry and White shirts from nearby Painswick R.F.C. way back in the late 1880s.

CONCEDING A CENTURY

The only season when Gloucester Rugby Football Club have conceded a century of points in a season was 1996-97. The playing record read as follows:

Played	Won	Drew	Lost	Points For	Points Against
42	23	1	18	1053	1005

CAPTAIN 'C'

Bob Clewes is the only player to have been appointed Captain with a surname beginning with the letter 'C'. Bob captained the Club in the 1997-98 season.

CLERIC

Mervyn Hughes, who became the Club Chairman was a former Cardiff cleric.

CLUB SCORING A THOUSAND POINTS

Season	Matches	Total	Captain
1972-73	53	1,145	John Bayliss
1973-74	54	1,096	Mike Nicholls
1975-76	53	1,105	Mike Burton
1976-77	51	1.147	John Watkins
1981-82	48	1,045	Steve Mills
1983-84	50	1,036	Gordon Sargent
1984-85	48	1,116	John Orwin
1988-89	45	1,030	Marcus Hannaford
1989-90	47	1,122	Mike Hamlin
1990-91	43	1,253	Mike Hamlin
1996-97	42	1,053	David Sims
1997-98	41	1,120	Peter Glanville
2001-02	35	1,274	Phil Vickery
2002-03	33	1,032	Phil Vickery

CENTURY MAKERS

When Gloucester Rugby Club defeated Bucharest at Kingsholm on 29th October 2005 the following players contributed to the 106 points scored with a sole penalty scored by the Romanian visitors. Ludovic Mercier and James Simpson-Daniel 20 points each, Rob Thirlby and Marcel Garvey 10 points each, Simon Amor 6, Andy Hazell, Haydn Thomas, Luke Narraway, Nick Wood, Anthony Allen, Adam Eustace and James Forrester 5 points each. A penalty try brought the total to 106 points.

CAPTAINS RECORD IN PROFESSIONAL RECORD

Season	Played	Won	Draw	Lost	Points For	Points Against	Captain
1996-1997	42	23	1	18	1,053	1005	D. Sims
1997-1998	41	23	1	17	1,120	946	P. Glanville
1998-1999	33	15	1	17	725	724	D. Sims
1999-2000	31	21	1	9	901	653	Kingsley Jones
2000-2001	33	16	1	16	719	770	Ian Jones
2001-2002	35	25	0	10	1,274	663	Phil Vickery

Season	Played	Won	Draw	Lost	Points For	Points Against	Captain
2002-2003	33	25	2	6	1.032	634	Phil Vickery
2003-2004	31	20	0	11	764	616	Jake Boer
2004-2005	33	16	1	16	650	692	Peter Buxton
2005-2006	34	22	1	11	996	542	Peter Buxton
2006-2007	33	21	2	10	861	687	Marco Botolami
2007-2008	33	21	1	11	820	596	Peter Buxton
2008-2009	33	19	0	14	680	656	Mike Tindall

CUP WINNERS – FIRST

The Gloucester team that defeated Northampton at Twickenham in the Powergen Cup Final of 2003 on 5th April:

T. Delport; M. Garvey, T. Fanolua, H. Paul, J. Simpson-Daniel; L. Mercier, A. Gommarsall; T. Woodman, O. Azam, A. Deacon, A. Eustace, R. Fidler, J. Boer (Captain), A. Hazell and J. Forrester.

LEAGUE CAREER RECORDS

Most points	848	Mark Mapletopt	1994-99
Most tries	44	James Simpson-Daniel	2001-08
Most conversions	122	Ludovic Mercier	2001-03/2005-07
Most penalties	183	Mark Mapletoft	1994-99
Most dropped goals	16	Ludovic Mercier	2001-03/2005-06

CODE CONVERTS

Two of the players who converted from Rugby League to Rugby Union and joined Gloucester Rugby Club eventually reverted to the thirteen man code. Karl Pryce who joined the Kingsholm staff from Bradford Bulldogs returned to his former club in 2007. Henry Paul left Kingsholm in 2006 to join Harlequins Rugby League team after his original move also from Bradford Bulls. In 2008 Henry decided once again to rejoin the fifteen man code when he signed a two-year contract with relegated Leeds Carnegie in National League One.

CAPTAINS RECORD IN AMATEUR ERA

Season	Played	Won	Drew	Lost	Points For	Points Against	Captain
1873-1874	3	3	–	–	–	–	F. Hartley
1874-75							F. Hartley
1875-76			No records available				F. Hartley
1876-77	11	6	2	3	NOT	KNOWN	J. F. Brown
1877-78	15	10	2	3	NOT	KNOWN	J. F. Brown
1878-79	15	10	2	3	NOT	KNOWN	J. F. Brown
1879-80	16	14	0	2	NOT	KNOWN	J. F. Brown
1880-81	13	7	3	3	NOT	KNOWN	J. F. Brown
1881-82	19	14	0	5	NOT	KNOWN	J. F. Brown
1882-83	14	11	3	0	NOT	KNOWN	J. F. Brown
1883-84	19	15	2	2	NOT	KNOWN	H. Broughton
1884-85	20	11	2	7	NOT	KNOWN	H. Broughton
1885-86	17	13	1	3	NOT	KNOWN	Tom Smith
1886-87	19	10	2	7	NOT	KNOWN	Tom Smith
1887-88	19	10	3	6	NOT	KNOWN	Tom Smith
1888-89	22	14	5	3	NOT	KNOWN	Tom Smith
1889-90	25	14	3	8	NOT	KNOWN	C. E. Brown
1890-91	26	21	3	2	NOT	KNOWN	Tom Bagwell
1891-92	32	23	3	6	317	94	Tom Bagwell
1892-93	29	15	2	12	168	141	Walter George
1893-94	28	18	1	9	234	185	J. Harman
1894-95	26	12	3	11	211	155	J. Harman
1895-96	27	9	6	12	140	165	C. Williams
1896-97	31	18	5	8	251	131	W. Taylor
1897-98	35	24	6	5	332	123	W. Taylor
1898-99	34	27	1	6	300	116	W. Taylor
1899-1900	31	22	2	7	401	112	W. Taylor
1900-01	34	24	5	5	522	75	G. Romans
1901-02	34	24	3	7	542	103	G. Romans
1902-03	34	19	1	14	366	186	G. Romans
1903-04	34	18	2	14	416	200	G. Romans

1904-05	37	24	2	11	522	158	G. Romans W. Johns
1905-06	37	26	3	8	661	165	W. Johns
1906-07	34	21	2	11	363	210	Dai Gent
1907-08	34	22	2	10	329	219	G. Vears
1908-09	36	22	4	10	437	236	A. Hudson
1909-10	38	24	7	7	412	191	A. Hudson
1910-11	40	25	2	13	488	187	A. Hudson
1911-12	40	24	4	12	364	261	A. Hudson
1912-13	40	21	4	15	363	230	G. Holford
1913-14	37	25	2	10	357	161	G. Holford
FIRST WORLD WAR							
1919-20	33	20	2	11	396	120	G. Holford
1920-21	37	25	2	10	454	261	F. Webb
1921-22	41	24	3	14	500	324	S. Smart
1922-23	42	28	3	11	519	261	F. Aycliffe
1923-24	39	24	1	14	426	310	T. Millington
1924-25	40	24	1	15	430	308	T. Voyce
1925-26	37	19	1	17	430	283	T. Voyce
1926-27	41	23	0	18	408	410	T. Voyce
1927-28	44	25	3	16	477	293	L. Saxby
1928-29	39	21	3	15	453	281	L. Saxby
1929-30	40	22	6	12	405	267	L. Saxby
1930-31	38	18	5	15	326	287	R. James
1931-32	37	19	3	15	282	262	L. Saxby
1932-33	37	24	3	10	423	257	A. Wadley
1933-34	37	27	2	8	497	191	A. Wadley
1934-35	39	25	0	14	550	315	A. Wadley
1935-36	37	23	5	9	402	233	J. Brooks
1936-37	36	20	2	14	342	247	D. Meadows
1937-38	36	29	1	6	413	228	J. A'Bear
1938-39	36	18	5	13	287	275	J. A'Bear
1939-40	20	10	5	5	291	196	Various
SECOND WORLD WAR							
1945-46	31	21	5	5	481	248	H. Boughton

1946-47	30	19	0	11	365	235	T. Price R. Morris
1947-48	40	29	1	10	588	292	G. Hudson
1948-49	43	23	5	15	429	288	G. Hudson
1949-50	43	19	7	17	295	277	G. Hudson
1950-51	45	23	6	16	373	248	T. Day
1951-52	45	30	4	11	563	316	J. Watkins
1952-53	43	24	4	15	435	331	B. Hodge
1953-54	43	32	1	10	452	286	J. Taylor
1954-55	41	19	3	19	392	402	G. Hastings
1955-56	42	15	4	23	363	380	P. Ford
1956-57	44	21	6	17	380	326	P. Ford
1957-58	44	26	3	15	382	335	P. Ford
1958-59	42	17	4	21	361	431	C. Thomas
1959-60	42	26	2	14	507	383	P. Ford
1960-61	48	18	8	22	409	439	P. Ford
1961-62	43	21	3	19	491	464	A. Townsend
1962-63	38	21	2	15	456	318	M. Booth
1963-64	44	27	3	14	507	340	A. Holder
1964-65	44	28	1	15	562	468	M. Booth
1965-66	49	23	6	20	444	421	M. Booth
1966-67	53	24	5	24	457	570	G. White
1967-68	55	23	7	25	581	520	D. Rutherford
1968-69	52	32	5	15	882	529	D. Smith
1969-70	57	31	1	25	761	619	D. Smith
1970-71	51	35	4	12	772	382	M. Nicholls
1971-72	49	37	3	9	821	414	M. Nicholls
1972-73	53	36	2	15	1145	636	J. Bayliss
1973-74	54	39	4	11	1096	576	M. Nicholls
1974-75	46	32	0	14	954	514	K. Richardson
1975-76	53	34	3	16	1105	627	M. Burton
1976-77	51	35	2	14	1147	530	J. Watkins
1977-78	49	38	0	11	993	501	J. Watkins
1978-79	48	35	2	11	798	455	J. Watkins
1979-80	50	34	4	12	884	464	R. Clewes

1980-81	51	37	2	12	931	551	S. Mills
1981-82	48	41	4	3	1045	338	S. Mills
1982-83	54	24	5	25	801	692	S. Mills
1983-84	50	33	1	16	1036	657	G. Sargent
1984-85	48	33	1	14	1116	534	J. Orwin
1985-86	47	33	0	14	1030	517	J. Orwin
1986-87	47	30	0	17	969	589	M. Preedy
1987-88	47	32	3	12	973	580	M. Hannaford
1988-89	45	34	1	10	1030	521	M. Hannaford
1989-90	47	34	2	11	1122	622	M. Hamlin
1990-91	43	32	0	11	1253	415	M. Hamlin
1991-92	40	29	1	10	844	478	I. Smith
1992-93	40	29	0	11	914	472	I. Smith
1993-94	41	22	2	17	849	609	I. Smith
1994-95	39	20	1	18	979	663	A. Deacon
1995-96	35	18	1	16	838	648	D. Sims

COLOURS

The affectionately called 'Cherry and White' colours were first worn in the 1894/95 season. In those days they were referred to as red and white. These colours were the fourth that Gloucester Rugby Football Club adopted since the Club was founded in 1873 by Francis Hartley.

The fifth set of club colours saw a thin band of black between the cherry hoops and the white hoops. The original club colours were black and mauve – this was because no other colours were readily available for the playing kit then! In the 1881/82 season came the dark blue jersey and for the first time, the City crest appeared in the colours. It was to be a lucky colour for at the end of the 1882/83 season it was the Club's only invincible season to date. At the end of the 14 match campaign the Club had recorded 11 wins and three draws.

The third set of club colours came in September 1886 when the Club were playing at the Spa. They then took to the field of play wearing red, yellow and black. They were to have been the Club's original colours in 1873 but were not available so it was in the 1994/95 season when Andy Deacon was Captain that there had been the first significant change for 100 years.

COURAGE LEAGUE STATISTICS

Played	Won	Drew	Lost	Points	Against	Tries	Scored
1987-88	10	6	1	3	206	121	32
1988-89	11	7	1	3	215	112	31
1989-90	11	8	1	2	214	139	32
1990-91	12	6	0	6	207	163	29
1991-92	12	7	1	4	193	168	19
1992-93	12	6	0	6	173	151	17
1993-94	18	6	2	10	247	356	21
1994-95	18	6	1	11	269	336	25
1995-96	18	6	0	12	275	370	20
1996-97	22	11	1	10	476	589	46
TOTALS	144	69	8	67	2475	2505	272

	MOST POINTS			MOST TRIES	
1987-88	42	Nick Marment		6	Jim Breeze
1988-89	85	Tim Smith		6	Mike Hamlin
1989-90	75	Tim Smith		6	Derek Morgan
1990-91	75	Tim Smith		4	Ian Smith, Derek Morgan, Paul Ashmead, Chris Dee
1991-92	81	Tim Smith		5	Simon Morris
1992-93	71	Tim Smith		3	Tim Smith, Derek Morgan
1993-94	82	Tim Smith		3	Paul Holford, Bruce Fenley
1994-95	85	Mark Mapletoft		8	Paul Holford
1995-96	79	Tim Smith		5	Paul Holford
1996-97	269	Mark Mapletoft		7	Mike Lloyd

CENTENARY TEAMS

When the Club played their Centenary match on Wednesday 4th October 1978 against Don Rutherford's International XV the teams lined up as:

Gloucester:
P. E. Butler; R. J. Clewes, T. Palmer, R. Jardine, R. Etheridge; R. L. Redwood,

J. H. Spalding; M. A. Burton, M. J. Nicholls (Captain), K. Richardson, P. J. Winnell, J. H. Fidler, J. A. Watkins, D. B. W. Owen and J. H. Haines.

International XV:
P. Villepreux (France); J. P. A. G. Jannion (England), J. S. Davis (Wales), J. Maso (France), D. J. Duckham (England); J. L. Berot (France), S. J. Smith (England); I. McLauchlan (Scotland), J. Young (Wales), A. B. Carmichael (Scotland), B. Dauga (France), C. W. Ralston (England), N. A. MacEwan (Scotland), M. Billiere (France) and A. Neary (England). The referee was R. F. Johnson (England).

A crowd of 9,000 witnessed a Gloucester victory by 24 points to 14.

CENTENARY DEFICIT

The Club Treasurer, Mr Doug Wadley, informed those who attended the Club's Annual General Meeting on Tuesday, July 9th 1974 that the Centenary Year had meant a loss of nearly £3,000, an excess income of £2,775 the previous year being turned into a deficit of £2,854. Those who attended were told the Club had been left with a 'Hadrian's Wall' of Centenary books they had been unable to sell! The Centenary dinner celebrations and expenses had cost the Club £3,968. Income from the game had been £3,124.

CENTENARY SHIRTS

The Club had specially made Centenary shirts; they were delayed in production due to delays in sewing on special badges. The International XV wore white jerseys bearing the Gloucester crest which were presented to the team in the Players room at the Kingsholm clubhouse. Special programmes and a Centenary book were on sale at the match.

A CHOICE FOR DON CASKIE

The former Gloucester R.F.C. centre three quarter who represented Scotland Under-21, Scottish students and Scotland B and is now a full time coach with National League Club, Moseley had soccer trials with Bristol City, Plymouth Argyle and Swindon Town before opting for Rugby Union.

CHEAP DAY RETURN!

In 1931 a cheap day return to London on Great Western Railway cost 12 shillings, equivalent to 60 pence in decimalisation, to watch a rugby match!

CENTENARY SEASON

Gloucester Rugby Football Club's centenary season ended with the third successive record of wins under the captaincy of hooker Mike Nicholls, 35 in 1970-1971, 37 in 1971-1972, and 39 in 1973-1974.

CIVIC RESPONSE

A civic reception was held at the end of the 1973/74 season on 2nd May to celebrate the centenary of the formation of the Club.

THE COURAGE TO START

The Courage League was introduced in 1987 and has since evolved into what we know today as the Guinness Premiership.

CUP SHARED

The Gloucester R.F.C. team that shared the honours with Moseley R.F.C. after a 12 points a piece draw on 1st May 1982 at Twickenham in the John Player Cup Final was:

P. Ford; P. Pritchard, P. A. Taylor, S. G. Parsloe, R. Mogg; L. Jones, S. J. W. Baker, M. Preedy, S. G. F. Mills (captain), P. J. Blakeway, S. B. Boyle, J. Orwin, J. Gadd, M. Teague and M. Longstaff.

Replacements: N. Price, G. Thomas, P. Wood, J. H. Fidler, G. A. F. Sargent and K. White.

COMPETITIONS

Gloucester Rugby Club have participated in the following competitions:

Gloucestershire County League
Leiden Euro Tournament in the Netherlands
Allied Dunbar Premiership   1997/98 – 1998/99
Zurich Premiership   1999/00 – 2004/05
Guinness Premiership   2005/06 – ?
Powergen KO Cup
Pilkington KO Cup
Tetleys Bitter KO Cup
John Player Cup
Anglo Welsh League
European Conference
Heineken European Cup
Cheltenham and Gloucester Cup
Boston Tournament
European Shield
European Challenge Cup
Zurich Wildcard
Courage Clubs Championship   1995/96 – 1996/97
Guinness Premiership Play-offs

COLLINS

There have been six players with the surname of Collins who have played
for Gloucester. They are A. Collins (1891-1894), F. Collins (1919), H. Collins
(1902-1907), S. Collins (1925), T. Collins (1891-1894), W. Collins (1920-
1924), W. Collins (1891-1896).

COOK

There have been 10 players with the surname of Cook who have appeared for
the Club's 1st XV. They are: A. Cook (1911-1913), B. V. Cook (1933-39), C.
Cook (1908-1920), G. Cook (1907), H. Cook (1911), J. Cook (1928), Jim Cook
(1897-1901), R. Cook (1922), Stan Cook (1910-1911) and T. Cook (1946).

CHAMPIONS

The Gloucester R.F.C. team that won the inaugural National Club Knock-Out
competition in the 1971-72 season, defeating Moseley by 17 points to six, was:
E. J. Stephens; R. J. Clewes, J. A. Bayliss, R. Morris, J. Dix; T. Palmer, M. H.

Booth; R. J. Cowling, M. J. Nicholls, (Captain), M. A. Burton, J. S. Jarrett, A. Brinn, J. A. Watkins, M. J. Potter, R. Smith.

Try Scorers:	J. Dix and R. Morris.
Drop Goals:	T. Palmer and M. H. Booth.
Penalty:	E. J. F. Stephens.

That season Gloucester R.F.C. defeated High Wycombe 40-6 in the Third Round on 23rd January. Then Exeter 34-3 in the Fourth Round on 27th February. Sale 13-6 in the Quarter Finals on 13th March and then Coventry 18-9 in the Semi Final on 3rd April.

CHELTENHAM AND GLOUCESTER

The Cheltenham and Gloucester League Cup was organised by the English Rugby Partnership and was designed to be a knockout cup for Clubs in the two Allied Dunbar Partnerships Leagues. The 1997-98 competition was the inaugural event and was backed by the C & G Building Society who committed £1 million over three years in sponsorship monies. There was a total prize fund of £120,000 with the winners receiving £20,000.

The teams that took part in the first season were Gloucester, Northampton, Wakefield, West Hartlepool, Fylde, Leicester, London Irish, Rotherham, Exeter, Orrell, Sale, Bristol, Moseley, Waterloo, Coventry, Bedford, Richmond, London Scottish, Blackheath and Cambridge University.

R.F.U. SENIOR CUP RECORD SEASON BY SEASON

1971-72 – Winners	1984-85 – Semi-Final	1996-97 – Semi-Final
1972-73 – 2nd Round	1985-86 – Quarter-Final	1997-98 – 5th Round
1973-74 – 2nd Round	1986-87 – Quarter-Final	1998-99 – Semi-Final
1974-75 – 2nd Round	1987-88 – 4th Round	1999-00 – Quarter Final
1975-76 – 2nd Round	1988-89 – Semi-Final	2000-01 – 5th Round
1976-77 – Quarter final	1989-90 – Runners-up	2001-02 – Quarter Final
1977-78 – Winners	1990-91 – 4th Round	2002-03 – Winners
1978-79 – 1st Round	1991-92 – Semi-Final	2003-04 – 6th Round
1979-80 – Quarter final	1992-93 – 3rd Round	2004-05 – Semi-Final
1980-81 – Quarter final	1993-94 – Quarter-Final	2005-06 – Group Stage
1981-82 – Shared	1994-95 – 4th Round	2006-07 – Group Stage
1982-83 – 3rd Round	1994-95 – 4th Round	2007-08 – Group Stage
1983-84 – Did Not Qualify	1995-96 – Semi-Final	2008-09 – Semi-Final

CAPPED BY ENGLAND

Phil Blakeway	was the – 1,061st player
Harold Boughton	was the – 712th player
Mike Burton	was the – 1,004th player
Peter Butler	was the – 1,028th player
Alf Carpenter	was the – 685th player
Peter Ford	was the – 921st player
Geroge Hastings	was the – 851st player
Arthur Hudson	was the – 423rd player
Don Rutherford	was the – 890th player
Dave Sims	was the – 1,205th player
Charles 'Wacker' Smith	was the – 362nd player
Christopher Tanner	was the – 665th player
Mike Teague	was the – 1,107th player
Phil Vickery	was the – 1,193rd player
Tom Voyce	was the – 563rd player
John Watkins	was the – 1,015th player

Line out during an early England versus Wales fixture

D

DIRECTION

The playing record of Gloucester Rugby Club under the various Directors of Rugby since the beginning of professionalism is as follows:

RICHARD HILL Overall				
Won	Drew	Lost	Points For	Points Against
40	3	43	1,997	2,123
Home				
32	2	11	1,138	750
Away				
12	1	32	859	1,373

PHILIPPE ST ANDRE Overall				
Won	Drew	Lost	Points For	Points Against
44	1	22	2,081	1,344
Home				
30	0	5	1,261	614
Away				
14	1	17	820	730

NIGEL MELVILLE Overall				
Won	Drew	Lost	Points For	Points Against
67	3	35	2,745	2,136
Home				
43	0	9	1,549	852
Away				
24	3	26	1,196	1,284

DEAN RYAN Overall				
Won	Drew	Lost	Points For	Points Against
83	4	45	3,325	2,476
Home				
54	1	11	1,928	1112
Away				
29	3	34	1,397	1,364

DIRECTORS

The Club's first Directors in 1891 were with appropriate shares in parenthesis:

A. W. Vears, Merchant (100), C. H. Priday, Land Agent (100), A. V. Hatton, Brewer (100), A. Woodward, Gentleman (50), G. Cumming, Malster (50), S. Davies, Haberdasher (25), T. Gurney, Builder (20), C. H. Dancey, No occupation (25).

DEFEAT

The first defeat at Kingsholm came in the 1891-92 season when Newport won by 2 points to nil.

DRAW

The first drawn match at Kingsholm also came in the 1891-92 season when Welsh visitors Penarth were participants in a pointless encounter.

DISRUPTION

'Disruptive elements' were causing an erosion of team spirit it was stated by the Club committee in 1955 and that rough play was creeping into the team and training sessions were not being attended.

ALL THE 'D's

Opponents have been: Derby, Devonport Albion, Devon Nomads, Devonport Services, Dewsbury, Dublin Wanderers, Dunvant and Devizes.

'OH DEAR'

Simon Deveraux was playing for Gloucester versus Rosslyn Park when he broke the jaw of the Rosslyn Park player, Jamie Cowie. He was charged with Grevious Bodily Harm and served a jail sentence of nine months.

DROPPED GOALS

Former Gloucester Rugby Football Club scrum half Mickey Booth holds the Club record for the most dropped goals in a career – 41. Willie Jones holds the Club record for the most dropped goals in a season – 17, 1947-48.

DISPOSED

In their successful European Challenge Cup triumph of 2006 the following clubs were defeated at Kingsholm – Bucharest (106-3), Toulon (66-5), Bayonne (32-19), Brive (46-13), Worcester (31-23). In away matches they remained undefeated – Bayonne (26-10), Toulon (74-3), Bucharest (27-13) and in the final at The Stoop home of the Harlequins R.F.C. against London Irish (36-34).

NATIONAL CUP WINNERS – 'D'

John Dix	1972
Andy Deacon	2003
Thinus Delport	2003

SIX OF THE DIX!

There were six members of the Dix family to have played for Gloucester, they were: Albert, John, Stuart, Thomas, William and Matthew. Father Dix was a scrum half and played for Gloucestershire when they defeated Yorkshire at Bradford in the final of the County Championship in 1920 by 27 points to 3.

John, Stuart and Clive Dix made appearances for the County, all grandsons of 'Father' Dix.

CAPTAINS 'D'

Players who have been appointed as Captains of this Club with their surname commencing with the letter 'D' are:

Tom Day	1950-51
Andy Deacon	1994-95

DAVIES X TWELVE'S

There have been twelve players with the surname of Davies who have appeared in the 1st XV. They are:

B. Davies (1946), D. Davies (1949), B. L. Davies (1945), Gwyn Davies (1929-30), J. Davies (1927-1931), L. Davies (1945), N. Davies (1945), S. H. Davies (1945-49), T. E. Davies (1958-1966), Bradley Davies (2003-2006), V. Davies (1949-1952) and M. Davies 2004-2007.

IS THERE A DOCTOR IN THE 'HOLM'?

There have been a quartet of medical practitioners who have appeared in the Club's 1st XV. They are a Dr Bryson who made a solitary appearance in 1929. Dr J. M. Dick added considerably to that sole match when he made 32 appearances between 1935 and 1937 scoring 2 tries and landing a drop goal. The quartet are complete when including Dr C. C. Taylor who made 34 appearances for the Club between 1924 and 1926 scoring 7 tries, adding three conversions and two dropped goals. Also Dr Steel-Perkins made 25 appearances between 1930 and 1931 scoring 5 tries and landing a solitary conversion.

HOMECOMING FOR DAVIES

Former Gloucester player, Glyn Davies appeared for the Club in 1945. He also appeared for the Army and Cambridge University and was capped 11 times by Wales when he joined Pontypridd.

DOUBLES

Up to the completion of the 2008-09 season we have completed the double (home and away) wins on 42 occasions since the advent of professional Rugby Union. They are as follows with home result first:

1996-97	West Hartlepool 37-10, 23-14, Orrell 30-0, 49-3, London Irish 29-19, 21-20	3
1997-98	Bristol 35-13, 14-13; Northampton 20-15, 24-22	2
1999-00	Sale 35-14, 31-13; Bristol 29-23, 38-25; London Irish 40-15, 42-40; Bedford 60-17, 18-6; Harlequins 24-23, 38-24	5
2000-01	Newcastle 28-13, 19-18; Rotherham 50-17, 29-28	2
2001-02	Sale 42-14, 44-21; Bristol 51-17, 41-40; Leeds 58-17, 50-17; Harlequins 33-7, 18-6	4
2002-03	Bristol 45-18, 38-21; Saracens 44-14, 29-22; London Irish 25-20, 40-19; Newcastle 25-23, 22-19; Harlequins 29-11, 25-19; Northampton 18-9,16-13	6
2003-04	Leicester 24-3, 28-18; Saracens 30-7, 16-8; Rotherham 22-8, 35-21, Harlequins 18-17, 16-0	4
2004-05	London Irish 23-16,13-12; Worcester 28-16, 18-13	2

2005-06	Saracens 21-12, 19-9; Newcastle 24-18, 13-9; Leeds 31-7, 31-7	3
2006-07	London Irish 15-3, 22-11; Northampton 28-27, 7-5; Worcester 33-19, 33-24; Harlequins 34-25, 31-26	4
2007-08	Wasps 27-21, 25-17; Saracens 23-12, 38-21; Newcastle 24-18, 20-13; Leeds 39-16, 49-24	4
2008-09	Bristol 39-10, 29-10; Saracens 22-16, 25-21	2

DRAWS

Gloucester Rugby Club have drawn 7 league matches in the professional era. The total amount in the league season by season is also included in the left hand column.

League		Gloucester Rugby Club	
1996-97	4	(1) Versus Bristol – Home – 26th April 1997	20-20
1997-98	4	(1) Versus Sale – Away – 30th December 1997	24-24
1998-99	8	(1) Versus Richmond – Home – 16th January 1999	24-24
1999-00	4	(0)	
2000-01	2	(0)	
2001-02	5	(0)	
2002-03	6	(2) Versus Bath – Away – 28th September 2002	21-21
		Versus Sale – Away – 18th April 2003	30-30
2003-04	7	(0)	
2004-05	5	(1) Versus Newcastle – Away – 27th February 2005	27-27
2005-06	7	(1) Versus Worcester – Away – 6th April 2006	15-15
2006-07	6	(2) Versus Leicester – Away – 16th September 2006	27-27
		Versus Bath – Away – 7th April 2007	21-21

In European competitions we have drawn 2 matches as follows:

European Shield

1999-2000	Versus Bridgend – Away – 11th December 1999	29-29

Heineken Cup

2000-2001	Versus Colomiers – Home – 21st October 2000	22-22

Domestic Competition – E.D.F. Energy Cup

2007-2008   Versus   Newcastle – Home – 27th October 2007   18-18

DOWNING STREET

Three Gloucester Rugby players were invited to No.10 Downing Street in
2003 to meet the Prime Minister, Tony Blair after England's 2003 World Cup
Victory in Australia, Andy Gomarsall, Phil Vickery and Trevor Woodman.

'DEACS' – THE FIRST

Prop forward Andy Deacon was the first Gloucester Rugby Club player to
be awarded a testimonial by the Club in recognition of his long service. Andy
spent 15 years at Kingsholm.

DIVINE INTERCEPTION

Gentlemen of the Holy cloth have been prevalent in Gloucester R.F.C. history
and recording them in alphabetical order we discover the following:

The Reverend Mervyn Hughes made 55 appearances for the 1st XV scoring 15
tries between 1937 and 1939. He later became the Club President. Reverend
D. James made just three first team appearances in 1945. In that same year of
1945, the Reverend A. T. Kembie made a solitary appearance.

The Reverend E. L. Phillips made a total of 56 first team appearances scoring
14 tries in the process between 1934 and 1936. The renowned Reverend
C. C. 'Kit' Tanner was a potent force at first team level by scoring 42 tries
from sixty-five first team matches between 1930 and 1937 and attaining full
International honours.

DIX IN THE MIX!

'Father Dix' of Gloucester Rugby Football Club who made 235 first team
appearances was a scrum half of International class. He scored 55 tries, kicked
10 conversions, one penalty and recorded eight drop goals in the years he spent
at Kingsholm 1907-1922. He was a member of the Gloucestershire County
team that defeated Yorkshire in the final of the Championship in 1920. His three
grandsons John, Stuart and Clive Dix all made appearances for the County team.

DOUBLE-BARRELLED

We are all familiar today with James Simpson-Daniel's name but how many other players have played for Gloucester 1st XV with the hyphen? There are a few:

J. Beresford-Smith made one appearance for the Club in 1945; D. Bruce-Jones made two appearances in 1924 scoring a try; Donald Crichton-Miller was a Scottish International who served the Club in 1929-1930 making 27 appearances and scoring 4 tries; D. Gilbert-Smith made 17 first team matches notching 4 tries between 1961 and 1962; E. Skinner-Jones played in four matches in 1895 kicking a sole conversion; Dr Steel-Perkins between 1930 and 1931 made 25 appearances scoring 5 tries, landing a conversion also. E. Triggs-Herbert played for the Club between 1923 and 1926 in which period he made 56 appearances and scored two tries.

In more modern times Rory Greenslade-Jones can be added to the list as can former scrum half Clive Stuart-Smith along with Herve Gregoire-Mazzocco.

Glorious Gloucester keep the flag flying

Gloucester 40
Northampton 22

PAUL ACKFORD
AT TWICKENHAM

First Lansdowne Road, now Twickenham. English rugby is going through the purplest of purple patches at the moment. This was another tremendous occasion played out in blinding sunshine in front of two fervent and marvellously partisan sets of supporters. Gloucester were deserved winners, powered home by James Simpson-Daniel and inspired by James Forrester. Behind at half-time, they surged back with a wonderful second-half performance of almost total dominance to send Northampton to their third Twickenham defeat in four years.

But, as important, it was another great day for the sport and another reason why the bigwigs of the International Rugby Board should give the 2007 World Cup to England when they vote in Dublin on Wednesday. If the English rugby public can get this excited over a club final heaven knows how they would respond if the World Cup came to town.

Most of the pre-match questions were aimed at Northampton. Savaged in last year's final by London Irish, it was unthinkable that they could capitulate again. Coach Wayne Smith designated two captains to lead them on to the pitch. "I want John Leslie and Budge Pountney to share in the responsibility of the final," Smith said. It was as if one man could not shoulder the burden alone.

And at the start of a tumultuous and turbulent first half it appeared as if the responsibility was too much even for two men. Northampton scored first through a Paul Grayson penalty but it was Gloucester who rattled the cage the hardest. At the restart, Gloucester's forwards drove ferociously, forcing Matt Dawson to fire a pass intended for Steve Thompson into no man's land where the swooping Simpson-Daniel snapped up the ball and strolled over for the try. When Ludovic Mercier added the conversion and a dropped goal six minutes later the prospect of another Northampton crumble was on.

But Northampton responded in a manner befitting a team comprising 14 internationals. North Harbour lock Matt Lord was their only non Test player, and he Dawson, Budge Pountney, Thompson and Ben Cohen combined to stabilise Northampton.

Grayson was just as influential in the early stages. He finished the half with 17 points and it was his break inside Mercier that set up the try for Nick Beal. Grayson is under intense scrutiny as the understudy to Jonny Wilkinson, but his early play when he mixed up his options was shrewd and accurate. And it would be foolish to make too much of the moment when he hauled down Mercier before the ball had arrived. Grayson was sent to the sin bin for that offence and the resultant penalty gave Gloucester an important lead at 30-22 going into the last quarter, but that aberration coincided with a spell during which Northampton could not put together an attack worthy of the name.

It was typical of the occasion and of the new-look Gloucester that they struck late in the first half through Marcel Garvey to get back into the match and were first to score after the break to edge ahead of Northampton. There was a time when Gloucester could not win away and one of the fears for them yesterday was that they

would be unable to repeat their Kingsholm form. That concern was heightened after 21 minutes when Rob Fidler was sent to the sin bin for talking back to the referee, Tony Spreadbury, but it is a mark of Gloucester's inner strength that they shrugged off Fidler's absence and regained the lead early in the second half.

Once again it was Forrester who produced the decisive move. Northampton made a mess of their scrummage when Andrew Blowers was caught

and Gloucester moved the ball right for the indecently quick Forrester to canter over in the corner. There was more than a hint of controversy to the score because television replays seemed to show that the Gloucester flanker did not have contact with the ball in the act of touching it down but none of the officials spotted it.

It was a good afternoon for Forrester, who has made star-tling progress up the rankings. He has presence and has shown that he does not fade on

the big occasion. Henry Paul was another to tickle the England selectors' fancies. The mastermind of England's sensational Hong Kong Sevens triumph, Paul was very tidy in the centre against Northampton.

That, in essence, was the difference between the two sides. Gloucester do not have the seasoned performers which Northampton can call upon. Bar a couple of oldies they are an outfit making their way in the game and it was Gloucester's collective energy and

desire which finally did for Northampton.

It was no coincidence that the final coup de théâtre occurred when Dawson, attempting to make something out of nothing and save the game, was interrupted by Mercier who found the flying Simpson-Daniel. Two big matches in a week was too much for Dawson and his England colleagues. All Gloucester were worried about was winning one game. They did and in some style.

Day tripper... Northampton's Ben Cohen is upended by Ludovic Mercier of Gloucester at Twickenham yesterday/Jamie McDonald

E

EUROPEAN CHALLENGE CUP

The Club were the Cup winners in 2006 when they defeated London Irish 36-34 at the Stoop, the home of Harlequins R.F.C.

EUROPE COMPETITION

The most points recorded by an individual in a single match in European competition are the 34 scored by Mark Mapletoft versus Ebbw Vale in the 1966/67 season in the European Conference.

'EDWARDS' PRAISE

The Club was praised by the civil dignitaries in 1882 when Alderman Edwards stated that they were providing an attraction for the working men and thus keeping them from public houses. This was the first season where the Club had remained unbeaten.

EXCURSION

An 'excursion' train was organised for the first time when the Club travelled to Cardiff in March 1890 by Great Western Railway.

EXCEPTIONAL!

In 1910 there were three Gloucester players selected by England to play against France – Arthur Hudson, William Johns and Henry Berry. They all appeared at the Parc des Princes on 3rd March. England winning by

11 points to three. Arthur Hudson scored two tries and Harold Berry the other!

CRAIG EMMERSON

The first English club to pay a transfer fee to another club was Gloucester when they signed Craig Emerson from northern club Moseley in 1996.

EXPECTANT ENGLAND

Seven England Under 21 players joined the Club in 1996. Richard Hill the Director of Rugby at Kingsholm held a coaching role with the England Under 21 team.

ELECTRIC

Electronic 'swipe cards' were introduced in 1997 for Season Ticket Holders.

ALL THE E's

Opponents have been: East Yorkshire Regiment, Ebbw Vale, England, Exeter and Exeter University.

A HIGH FOR ENGLAND

England's score of 36 points against Ireland at Lansdowne Road on 12 February 1938 was their highest in an International between the Great War and the Second World War. Graham Parker, the former Gloucester Rugby Football Club kicked six conversions equalling the England match record.

EXODUS

Following the advent of the professional era in the game of Rugby Union, Bath R.F.C. has witnessed an exodus of players that have found their way to Kingsholm, not all by a direct route. Those who have eventually arrived in this fair city are:

Ed Pearce, Steve Ojomoh, Audley Lumsdon, Mike Tindall, Iain Balshaw, Olly Barkley, Alex Brown, Henry Paul, Rob Thirlby, Gareth Cooper, Gareth Delve, Trevor Woodman, Dave Timmington, Andy Gomarsall, Neil McCarthy, Ian Sanders, Mike Lloyd and Olly Barkley.

Movement in the other direction, Kingsholm to the Recreation Ground is more muted. Those who have moved south have been:

Terry Hopson (who later rejoined Gloucester), Rob Fidler and Terry Sigley.

DANNY EVANS

Danny Evans was capped by Wales whilst playing for Cardiff University in 1934 versus England. The diminutive scrum half only made this sole appearance for his country at Cardiff Arms Park. Percy Hordern was included in the England XV that won by 9 points to nil. Danny made 81 appearances in the post war years 1945-1948 scoring 4 tries for his Club. Danny also played County Championship rugby for Cheshire.

EUROPE AT WAR

Francis Edwards, the Wycliffe centre was Gloucester's only representative in the England team named to meet Wales on 13th April 1940 as Kingsholm prepared for its first International fixture for 40 years. Interesting to note that Gloucester was still being referred to as the 'City' as late as the 1960s.

NATIONAL CUP WINNER – E

Adam Eustace   2003

ENGLAND INTERNATIONAL

A total of 62 players have represented England whilst playing for Gloucester. The first was Frank Stout in 1897.

Three Gloucester players were in the 2003 World Cup winning squad in Australia in 2003: Andy Gomarsall, Phil Vickery and Trevor Woodman. Both Vickery and Woodman played in the Final.

Phil Vickery is the Club's most capped players with 47 caps and he became the first player from Gloucester Rugby Club to captain England.

E

England International

Anthony Allen	2006-	2 caps
Iain Balshaw	2006	11 caps
Scott Benton	1998	1 cap
Henry Berry	1910	4 caps
Phil Blakeway	1980-1985	19 caps
Harold Boughton	1935	3 caps
Stephen Boyle	1983	3 caps
Alan Brinn	1972	3 caps
Alex Brown	2006-	3 caps
Mike Burton	1972-1978	17 caps
Peter Butler	1975-1976	2 caps
Alfred Carpenter	1932	1 cap
John Fidler	1981-1984	4 caps
Robert Fidler	1998	2 caps
Peter Ford	1964	4 caps
James Forrester	2005	2 caps
David Gent	1905-1910	5 caps
Andy Gomarsall	2000-2004	17 caps
Phil Greening	1996-1997	3 caps
Charles Hall	1901	2 caps
George Hastings	1955-1958	13 caps
Andy Hazell	2004-	6 caps
George Holford	1920	2 caps
William Hook	1951-1952	3 caps
Percy Hordern	1934	1 cap
Arthur Hudson	1906-1910	8 caps
William Johns	1909-1910	7 caps
Peter Kingston	1975-1979	5 caps
Maurice McCanlis	1931	2 caps
Mark Mapletoft	1997	1 cap
Neil McCarthy	1999-2000	3 caps
Steve Mills	1981-1984	5 caps
Oliver Morgan	2007-	2 caps
Luke Narraway	2008-	7 caps
Steve Ojomoh	1998	1 cap
John Orwin	1985	7 caps
Grahame Parker	1938	2 caps
Henry Paul	2002-2004	6 caps
Malcolm Preedy	1984	1 cap
Tom Price	1948	2 caps

Donald Rutherford	1965-1967	9 caps
Peter Richards	2006-2007	6 caps
Gordon Sargent	1981	1 cap
Lesley Saxby	1932	2 caps
James Simpson-Daniel	2002-	8 caps
David Sims	1998	3 caps
Sidney Smart	1913-1920	12 caps
Charles Smith	1901	1 cap
Frank Stout	1897-1899	7 caps
Percy Stout	1898-1899	5 caps
Christopher Tanner	1930-1932	5 caps
Mike Teague	1985-1991	22 caps
Mike Tindall	2005-	20 caps
Phil Vickery	1998-2005	47 caps
Lesley Vainikolo	2008-	5 caps
Tom Voyce	1920-1926	27 caps
John Watkins	1972-1975	7 caps
Richard West	1995	1 caps
Chris Williams	1976	1 cap
Ken Wilson	1963	1 cap
Alf Wood	1908	3 caps
Trevor Woodman	1999-2004	21 caps

EUROPEAN COMPETITIONS

Gloucester Rugby Club has participated in the following European Cup competitions:

European Conference	1996-97, 1997-98
European Shield	1999-00, 2001-02
Heineken Cup	2000-01, 2002-03, 2003-04, 2004-05, 2006-07, 2007-08, 2008-09
European Challenge Cup	2005-06 (winners)

EUROPE'S BEST

A report issued in March 2008 placed the Club as one of the best supported in Europe, based on league matches only.

1	Stade Francais	25,959
2	Toulouse	19,186
3	Leicester	17,116
4	Clermont Auvergne	14,034
5	Gloucester	13,860
6	Leinster	13,335
7	Toulon	12,727
8	Bayonne	12,679
9	Perpignan	11,640
10	Northampton	11,409
11	London Irish	10,506
12	Harlequins	10,472
13	Bath	10,450

The worst supported club? Glasgow – 1,823.

EXILES

The first of the Exiles to visit Kingsholm were London Scottish in 1891/92. A 2-0 win ensued for the 'City'. Then in the 1901-02 season London Welsh were beaten 14-3. It was not until November 1973 that London Irish visited Kingsholm. The Irish were defeated by 27 points to nine.

EUROPEAN COMPETITION

The highest points score was a 106 versus Bucharest at Kingsholm on 29th October 2005.

The biggest winning margin was by 103 points when Bucharest were defeated at Kingsholm by 106 points to three.

The highest score against Gloucester was the 62 points recorded by Swansea on 19th October 1996.

The largest losing margin inflicted was by 50 points in the 62 points to twelve defeat at St Helens, Swansea on 19th October 1996.

The most tries scored in a match is held jointly by Daren O'Leary who recorded 5 tries versus Gran Parma on 5th January 2002 at Kingsholm and Tom Beim who also scored 5 tries versus Viadana on 18th October 2000 at Stadio Zafanella.

The most conversions kicked in a match were by Henry Paul versus Gran Parma when he kicked 12 conversions on 5th January 2002 at Kingsholm.

The most penalties in a match were recorded by Ludovic Mercier when he kicked 6 penalties versus Ebbw Vale on 25th January 2002.

The most drop goals in a match were also recorded by Ludovic Mercier when he dropped 2 goals versus La Rochelle on 12th January 2002 at Stade Marcel, Defiandre.

ENGLISH CHAMPIONS LEAGUE TABLES

1987/1988	Leicester	1998/1999	Leicester
1988/1989	Bath	1999/2000	Leicester
1989/1990	Wasps	2000/2001	Leicester
1990/1991	Bath	2001/2002	Leicester
1991/1992	Bath	2002/2003	Gloucester
1992/1993	Bath	2003/2004	Bath
1993/1994	Bath	2004/2005	Leicester
1994/1995	Leicester	2005/2006	Sale
1995/1996	Bath	2006/2007	Gloucester
1996/1997	Bath	2007/2008	Gloucester
1997/1998	Newcastle	2008/2009	Leicester

From 2002-03 until 2004-05 the top three teams in the final league standings played for this trophy. 2nd placed played 3rd placed in a semi-final with the winner playing the 1st placed team.

In 2005-06 this changed to the top four teams, with 1st versus 4th and 2nd versus 3rd in the semi-finals, home advantage given to 1st and 2nd.

WINNER

2002-03	London Wasps
2003-04	London Wasps
2004-05	London Wasps
2005-06	Sale Sharks
2006-07	Leicester Tigers
2007-08	London Wasps
2008-09	Leicester Tigers

EUROPEAN OPPOSITION

The following clubs have been played in European Competitions under the various guises:

European Conference

Ebbw Vale, Begles Bordeaux, Swansea, Bourgoin, London Irish, Padova, Toulon, Beziers and Stade Francais.

European Challenge Cup

Bayonne, Bucceresti, Toulon, Brive, Worcester and London Irish.

European Shield

Biarritz, Spain, Bridgend, La Rochelle, Gran Parma, Caerphilly and Sale.

Heineken European Cup

Bayonne, Bucharest, Toulon, Brive, Worcester, London Irish, Llanelli, Roma, Colomiers, Leicester, Munster, Viadana, Perpignan, Treviso, Bourgoin, Wasps, Stade Francais, Ulster, Cardiff, Leinster, Agen, Edinburgh, Ospreys, Biarritz and Calvisano.

EUROPEAN – RESULTS AT KINGSHOLM

Competition	Date	Result	Opponents	Attendance
Heineken European Cup	12th October 2002	Won 35-16	Munster	11,000
	3rd December 2002	Won 33-16	Perpignan	8,112
	11th January 2003	Won 64-16	Viadana	8,271
Heineken European Cup	13th December 2003	Won 49-13	Bourgoin	9,492
	10th January 2004	Won 22-11	Munster	11,000
	31st January 2004	Won 42-11	Treviso	10,717

Competition	Date	Result	Opponents	Attendance
Heineken European Cup	30th October 2004	Won 55-13	Ulster	12,487
	4th December 2004	Won 23-19	Cardiff	11,795
	16th January 2005	Lost 0-27	Stade Francais	13,000
European Challenge Cup	29th October 2005	Won 106-3	Buccaresti	8,806
	17th December 2005	Won 66-5	Toulon	9,037
	21st January 2006	Won 32-19	Bayonne	8,582
	1st April 2006	Won 46-13	Brive	6,898
	22nd April 2006	Won 31-23	Worcester	8,609

Competition	Date	Result	Opponents	Attendance
Heineken European Cup	28th October 2006	Lost 26-32	Agen	10,134
	9th December 2006	Won 38-22	Edinburgh	9,749
	19th January 2007	Won 19-13	Leinster	12,500
Heineken European Cup	16th November 2007	Won 26-18	Ospreys	16,226
	15th December 2007	Won 51-27	Bourgoin	12,370
	20th January 2008	Won 29-21	Ulster	12,480
	5th April 2008	Lost 3-6	Munster	16,500
	11th October 2008	Won 22-10	Biarritz	11,273
	13th December 2008	Won 48-5	Calvisano	13,970
	18th January 2009	Lost 12-16	Cardiff	14,916

EMMS – NICE TRY

Former Gloucester Rugby Club prop forward Simon Emms lost his legal attempt in 2008 to claim tax back on some of the 4,500 calories he consumed each day. He argued that protein shakes and supplements should be tax deductable. Simon was playing for Northampton in the 2007-2008 season. He played on loan to Gloucester Rugby Club in the 2004-2005 season making his one league appearance at Kingsholm versus Newcastle in a 31 points to seventeen victory.

EUROPEAN RESULTS and POINTS SCORERS

Season	Competition	Opponents	Result	Date	Attendance	Venue
1996/ 1997 European Conference		Ebbw Vale	Won 59-7	12th October		Home
		Try Scorers: M. Mapletoft (4), E. Anderson, A. Lumsden, A. Saverimutto, S. Deveraux, Penalty Try Conversions: M. Mapletoft (7)				
		Begles Bordeaux	Lost 10-17	16th October		Home
		Try Scorers: Penalty Try Conversions: M. Mapletoft Penalty: M. Mapletoft				
		Swansea	Lost 12-62	19th October		Away
		Penalties: A. Morris (4)				
		Bourgoin	Lost 9-24	27th October		Home
		Penalties: M. Mapletoft (3)				
		London Irish	Won 29-13	2nd November		Away
		Try Scorers: P. Greening (2), A. Lumsden (2), A. Saverimutto Conversions: M. Mapletoft (2)				

Season	Competition	Opponents	Result	Date	Attendance	Venue
1997/ 1998 European Conference		Padova	Won 43-10	7th September	4,151	Home
		Try Scorers: P. Glanville (3), P. St. Andre, R. St. Andre, C. Emmerson Conversions: M. Mapletoft (5)				
		Toulon	Won 18-15	13th September	4,309	Home
		Penalties: M. Mapletoft (4) Drop Goals: M. Mapletoft (2)				
		Bezier	Won 29-27	20th September	3,000	Away
		Try Scorers: P. Glanville, P. Greening, T. Windo Conversion: M. Mapletoft Penalties: M. Mapletoft (4)				
		Toulon	Lost 13-16	27th September	6,431	Away
		Try Scorer: P. Greening Conversion: M. Mapletoft (3) Penalties: M. Mapletoft (2)				

Bezier	Won 38-17	4th October	4,548	Home
Try Scorers: P. St. Andre (2), C. Catling, M. Mapletoft Conversions: M. Mapletoft Penalties: M. Mapletoft (4)				
Padova	Won 29-16	12th October	2,000	Away
Try Scorers: P. St. Andre, S. Benton, P. Glanville, T. Fanolua, N. Osman, E. Pearce Conversions: T. Fanolua (2)				
Stade Francais	Lost 22-53	8th November	7,513	Away
Try Scorers: A. Lumsden, N. Osman, Penalty Try Conversions: T. Fanolua (2) Penalty: T. Fanolua				

1998/ 1999	No entry

Season	Competition	Opponents	Result	Date	Attendance	Venue
1999/ 2000 European Shield		Biarritz	Won 22-13	11th November	3,218	Home
		Try Scorers: R. Fidler, B. Johnson Penalties: C. Catling (2), M. Kimber (2)				
		Spain	Won 42-19	27th November	2,000	Away
		Try Scorers: B. Johnson 2, C. Catling, T. Glassie, R. Jewell, K. Jones. Conversions: T. Fanolua 3 Penalties: T. Fanolua 2				
		Bridgend	Drew 29-29	11th December	1,200	Away
		Try Scorers: C. Collins, J. Ewens, I. Sanders, Penalty Try Conversions: S. Mannix (3) Penalty: S. Mannix				
		Bridgend	Won 23-6	18th December	3,000	Home
		Try Scorers: B. Johnson, J. Ewens, M. Cornwell Conversions: T. Fanolua Penalties: T. Fanolua (2)				
		Spain	Won 47-7	8th January	3,361	Home
		Try Scorers: T. Glassie (2), D. Djoudi, T. Fanolua, B. Johnson Conversions: T. Fanolua (3), S. Mannix (2) Penalties: T. Fanolua (2), S. Mannix (2)				
		Biarritz	Lost 25-39	15th January	5,000	Away
		Try Scorers: T. Glassie (2), N. McCarthy, R. Tombs Conversions: T. Fanolua Penalty: T. Fanolua				

Season	Competition	Opponents	Result	Date	Attendance	Venue
		Llanelli	Won 27-20	6th October	7,000	Away
		Try Scorers: A. Hazell, J. Little Conversion: A. Gomarsall Penalties: S. Mannix (3) T. Fanolua (2)				
		Roma	Won 52-12	14th October	5,000	Home
		Try Scorers: T. Beim (5), F. Schisano Conversions: T. Fanolua (3), E. Moncreiff (2) Penalties: E. Moncreiff (4)				
		Colomiers	Drew 22-22	21st October	5,325	Home
		Try Scorers: Penalty Try Conversion: B. Hayward Penalties: E. Moncreiff (5)				
2000/ 2001 Heineken Cup		Colomiers	Lost 19-30	28th October	3,500	Away
		Try Scorer: C. Catling Conversion: S. Mannix Penalties: S. Mannix (4)				
		Llanelli	Won 28-27	13th January	10,500	Home
		Try Scorers: Penalty Try Conversion: S. Mannix Penalties: S. Mannix (6) Drop Goal: E. Moncreiff				
		Roma	Won 38-29	20th January	1,200	Away
		Try Scorers: J. Ewens, J. Little Conversion: S. Mannix (2) Penalties: S. Mannix (8)				
		Cardiff	Won 21-15	27th January	10,500	Home
		Penalties: S. Mannix (6), B. Hayward				
		Leicester (played at Vicarage Road)	Lost 15-19	21st April	14,010	Away
		Penalties: S. Mannix (5)				

Season	Competition	Opponents	Result	Date	Attendance	Venue
2002/2003 Heineken Cup		Munster	Won 35-16	12th October	11,000	Home
		Try Scorers: J. Boer (2), M. Garvey, L. Mercier Conversions: L. Mercier (3) Penalties: L. Mercier (3)				
		Viadana	Won 80-23	18th October	1,750	Away
		Try Scorers: T. Fanolua (3), J. Simpson-Daniel (3), H. Paul (2), J. Boer, M. Garvey, J. Forrester, R. Roncero. Conversions: L. Mercier (10)				
		Perpignan	Won 33-16	3rd December	8,112	Home
		Try Scorers: M. Garvey (2), L. Mercier. Conversions: L. Mercier (3) Penalties: L. Mercier (4)				
		Perpignan	Lost 23-31	11th December	7,500	Away
		Try Scorers: J. Boer, L. Mercier Conversions: L. Mercier (2) Penalties: L. Mercier (3)				
		Viadana	Won 64-16	11th January	8,271	Home
		Try Scorers: J. Paramore (2), R. Todd (2), T. Beim, M. Garvey, T. Fanolua, O. Azam, J. Forrester, C. Collins Conversions: L. Mercier (7)				
		Munster	Lost 6-33	18th January	14,000	Away
		Penalties: L. Mercier (2)				

Season	Competition	Opponents	Result	Date	Attendance	Venue
2003/2004	Heineken Cup	Treviso	Won 33-12	6th December	3,000	Away
		Bourgoin	Won 49-13	13th December	9,492	Home
		Munster	Won 22-11	10th January	11,000	Home
		Munster	Lost 14-35	17th January	12,000	Away
		Bourgoin	Won 37-13	24th January	6,000	Away
		Treviso	Won 42-11	31st January	10,717	Home
		Wasps	Lost 3-34	11th April	10,000	Away

Try Scorers: J. Paramore (2), A. Eustace, J. Simpson-Daniel
Conversions: H. Paul (2)
Penalties: H. Paul (3)

Try Scorers: J. Simpson-Daniel (2), A. Eustace, M. Garvey, T. Fanolua, H. Paul
Conversions: H. Paul (5)
Penalties: H. Paul (3)

Try Scorer: J. Simpson-Daniel
Conversion: H. Paul
Penalties: H. Paul (4)
Drop Goal: H. Paul

Try Scorer: J. Goodridge
Penalties: H. Paul (3)

Try Scorers: M. Garvey, D. McRae, H. Paul, J. Simpson-Daniel
Conversions: H. Paul (4)
Penalties: H. Paul (3)

Try Scorers: P. Buxton, J. Goodridge, M. Garvey, R. Todd, J. Simpson-Daniel, Penalty Try
Conversion: H. Paul (6)

Penalty: H. Paul

Season	Competition	Opponents	Result	Date	Attendance	Venue
2004-05 Heineken Cup		Stade Francais	Lost 31-39	23rd October	11,800	Away
		Try Scorers: J. Simpson-Daniel (2), J. Forrester Conversions: H. Paul (2) Penalties: H. Paul (4)				
		Ulster	Won 55-13	30th October	12,487	Home
		Try Scorers: M. Garvey, J. Goodridge, C. Buezenhout, A. Balding, D. McRae, J. Simpson-Daniel Conversions: H. Paul (5) Penalties: H. Paul (4) Drop Goal: H. Paul				
		Cardiff	Won 23-19	4th December	11,795	Home
		Try Scorers: T. Fanolua (2), J. Bailey Conversion: H. Paul Penalties: H. Paul (2)				
		Cardiff	Won 23-16	11th December	10,186	Away
		Try Scorers: T. Fanolua (2), J. Bailey Conversion: H. Paul Penalties: H. Paul (2)				
		Ulster	Lost 12-14	7th January	11,435	Away
		Penalties: H. Paul (3) Drop Goal: S. Amor				
		Stade Francais	Draw 0-0	16th January	13,000	Home
		No Points				

Season	Competition	Opponents	Result	Date	Attendance	Venue
2006-07 Heineken Cup		Leinster	Lost 20-37	21st October	22,530	Away
		Try Scorers: J. Adams, M. Foster Conversions: R. Lamb (2) Penalties: R. Lamb (3)				
		Agen	Lost 26-32	28th October	10,134	Home
		Try Scorers: A. Allen (2), O. Azam Conversion: W. Walker Penalties: R. Lamb (3)				
		Edinburgh	Won 38-22	9th December	9,749	Home
		Try Scorers: A. Allen, O. Azam, M. Foster, M. Tindall, J. Simpson-Daniel Conversions: W. Walker (2) Penalties: R. Lamb, W. Walker Drop Goal: W. Walker				
		Edinburgh	Won 31-14	17th December	4,125	Away
		Try Scorers: A. Allen, O. Morgan, L. Narraway, M. Tindall Conversions: W. Walker (3), R. Lamb Penalty: R. Lamb				
		Agen	Lost 18-26	12th January	5,000	Away
		Try Scorers: I. Balshaw, P. Richards Conversion: R. Lamb Penalties: R. Lamb (2)				
		Leinster	Won 19-13	19th January	12,500	Home
		Try Scorers: C. Califano, M. Foster Penalty Try Conversions: R. Lamb, W. Walker				

Season	Competition	Opponents	Result	Date	Attendance	Venue
2007-08 Heineken Cup		Ulster	Won 32-14	9th November	13,000	Away
		Try Scorers: I. Balshaw, R. Lamb, M. Tindall, J. Simpson-Daniel, L. Vainikolo Conversions: R. Lamb (2) Penalty: R. Lamb				
		Ospreys	Won 26-18	16th November	16,226	Home
		Try Scorers: A. Allen, J. Simpson-Daniel Conversions: R. Lamb, C. Paterson Penalties: R. Lamb (3), C. Paterson				
		Bourgoin	Won 31-7	7th December	6,500	Away
		Try Scorers: A. Allen, R. Lamb, J. Simpson-Daniel, A. Titterell Conversions: R. Lamb (4) Penalty: R. Lamb				
		Bourgoin	Won 51-27	15th December	12,370	Home
		Try Scorers: I. Balshaw, G. Delve, R. Lamb, A. Qera, L. Vainikolo, W. Walker Conversions: R. Lamb (6) Penalties: R. Lamb (3)				
		Ospreys	Lost 15-32	12th January	18,017	Away
		Try Scorers: R. Lamb, R. Lawson Conversion: C. Paterson Penalty: R. Lamb				
		Ulster	Won 29-21	20th January	12,480	Home
		Try Scorers: A. Qera (2), I. Balshaw, L. Narraway, A. Strokosch Conversions: C. Paterson (2)				
		Munster	Lost 3-16	5th April	16,500	Home
		Penalty: R. Lamb				

Season	Competition	Opponents	Result	Date	Attendance	Venue
2008-09 Heineken Cup		Biarritz	Won 22-10	11th October	11,723	Home
		Try Scorer: J. Simpson-Daniel Conversion: O. Barkley Penalties: O. Barkley (4), R. Lamb				
		Cardiff	Lost 24-37	19th October	27,141	Away
		Try Scorers: I. Balshaw (2), O. Morgan Conversions: O. Barkley (3) Penalty: O. Barkley				
		Calvisano	Won 40-17	6th December	3,700	Away
		Try Scorers: R. Lamb, M. Bortolami, M. Foster, L. Narraway, M. Tindall, Penalty Try Conversions: O. Barkley (5)				
		Calvisano	Won 48-5	13th December	13,970	Home
		Try Scorers: M. Watkins (2), L. Vainikolo (2), L. Narraway, M. Foster Conversions: R. Lamb (6) Penalties: R. Lamb (2)				
		Cardiff	Lost 12-16	18th January	14,916	Home
		Penalties: O. Barkley (4)				
		Biarritz	Lost 10-24	23rd January	7,000	Away
		Try Scorer: J. Simpson-Daniel Conversion: O. Barkley Penalty: O. Barkley				

F

FLOODLIGHTS

The first match played under floodlights at Kingsholm was in November 1967 when Gloucester Rugby Club entertained Bosuns whom they defeated 34-8. The Bosuns were a team comprised of players form various clubs.

FIDLERS IN UNISON

Neither John nor Robert Fidler were awarded an International Cap by England that would have enabled them to represent their country in a home fixture. John was awarded four caps and Rob two, all in away fixtures.

FATHER AND SON

John and Robert Fidler are the only father and son combination to have represented England at International level from Gloucester R.F.C.

FIRST

Three players from Gloucester Rugby Football Club were selected to play in the first International match played at Twickenham on 15th January 1910 versus Wales. They were Henry Berry, 'Dai' Gent and William Johns.

A FOOTBALL CLUB!

In 1873 Gloucester Football Club, as it was then known was formed in September, it was announced in the Gloucester Journal on the 13th of the month: 'A meeting will be held at the Spread Eagle Hotel on Monday evening at half past seven for the purpose of enrolling members of a football club when a committee, captain and other officers will be appointed. Persons wishing to become members will please attend: J. P. Riddiford. Secretary. Pro Term 9th Sep 1873'.

FRONT ROW

The entire front row forwards who faced South Africa on 2nd June 1984 in Port Elizabeth for England were Gloucester R.F.C. players namely – Philip Blakeway, Stephen Mills and Malcolm Preedy. The Springboks won 33-15.

FREEDOM OF CITY

Following England's World Cup success in Australia in 2003 three Gloucester players were granted the freedom of the City of Gloucester: Andrew Gomarsall, Philip Vickery and Trevor Woodman.

FIRST MEETING

Our first meeting with the current Guinness Premiership Clubs stretches over a century or more, they are as follows:

		HOME	AWAY
Bath	1896	0-0	3-3
Bristol	24th Sept 1892	14-0	2-2
Harlequins	1913	8-8	–
Leeds	21st Dec 1996	55-20	–
Leicester	Oct 1891	6-0	15-0
Northampton	1st April 1899	18-8	–
Newcastle (Gosforth)	1978	19-10	–
Sale	18th April 1933	18-7	–
Saracens	1968	3-3	–
London Irish	1973	27-9	–
Wasps	1946	8-5	–
Worcester	1999	31-17	–

A proud record where we were never defeated on any occasion.

THAT MAN FORD

Former Gloucester and England back row forward, Peter Ford, scored a club record of 146 tries. This is the highest total for a forward in the Club's history.

THE FIRST FOUR

There were four fixtures played in the first season. The first game was versus College School. Matches were played at the Spa, which was owned by the Gloucester Cricket Club and sub-let to Gloucester Football Club during winter months.

FOOTBALL

The first evidence of 'football' as rugby was called in those times was of matches being played at the Spa ground.

FLOODLIGHTS AT THE SPA

The first floodlight match the Club played was on 30th January 1879 when Rocklease who were based in Bristol met Gloucester Football Club in front of an attendance of 2,000 spectators.

FIRST TUESDAY

On 16th September 1873 it was announced 'A football club has been formed in the city – the season's operations began at the Spa on the first Tuesday in next month'.

FAILING TO SCORE

Failing to register a point at Kingsholm appears to the modern day supporter to be almost an impossibility but there was a period in the Club's history where it was almost commonplace. Those scoreless matches were as follows:

1891-1892	Penarth
1894-1895	Leicester
1895-1896	Swansea – Old Merchant Taylors – Bath
1896-1897	Cinderford
1897-1898	Llanelli – Newport
1899-1900	Leicester
1900-1901	Newport – Old Merchant Taylors
1901-1902	Newport
1904-1905	Devonport Albion
1908-1909	Swansea
1909-1910	Neath
1921-1922	Swansea
1922-1923	Pontypool
1924-1925	Lydney
1930-1931	Lydney – Llanelli
1936-1937	Bristol
1938-1939	Llanelli
1949-1950	Llanelli
1950-1951	Cheltenham – Bristol
1951-1952	Stroud
1955-1956	Swansea
1956-1957	Cheltenham
1960-1961	Old Blues
1966-1967	Coventry
1976-1977	London Scottish

All these matches resulted in 0-0 encounters

ALL THE 'F's

Four players with their surname beginning with the letter 'F' have played for England: John and Robert Fidler, Peter Ford and James Forrester.

FIDLER AT THE HELM

John Fidler, the former England lock forward was the Club's first team Manager and then Secretary from 1991 to March 2002.

OPPONENTS – F

Opponents have been: Fenners XV, First Gloucester, Forest of Dean Combination, French Universities, and Fylde.

THE FIRST VISITORS

The first season of activity on the playing field at Kingsholm saw the following teams appear with the following results in the 1891-92 season:

Burton On Trent	Won	18-0
St Helens Recreation	Won	6-0
Old Edwardians	Won	28-0
Newport	Lost	0-2
Swansea	Won	5-0
Coventry	Won	12-0
Leicester	Won	6-0
Dewsbury	Lost	0-7
Wakefield	Won	24-8
Moseley	Won	9-0
Penarth	Drew	0-0
Cardiff	Won	2-0
Exeter	Won	13-0
Maritime	Drew	2-2
London Scottish	Won	2-0
Barbarians	Won	10-9
Lydney	Won	26-0
Devonport Albion	Won	17-2
Rest Of County	Won	19-6
Devon Nomads	Won	15-0
Troedyrhiw	Won	22-2
Penarth	Won	15-0

Amazingly in the first eight matches either Gloucester or the visitors failed to score a point! Even after the visit of Wakefield, a further five matches produced the same phenomenon. In total, 16 matches produced no points for either club playing.

Adam Eustace.
© Andy Davey

Akapusi Qera.
© Andy Davey

ALASDAIR
STROKOSCH

Alasdair Strokosch.
© Andy Davey

ALEX
BROWN

Alex Brown.
© Andy Davey

Alasdair Dickinson.
© Andy Davey

Andy Hazell.
© Andy Davey

Andy Titterrell.
© Andy Davey

Anthony Allen.
© Andy Davey

Carlos Nieto.
© Andy Davey

Dave Young.
© Andy Davey

Dean Ryan.
© Andy Davey

Gareth Cooper.
© Andy Davey

Gareth Delve.
© Andy Davey

Ian Balshaw.
© Andy Davey

Jack Adams.
© Andy Davey

Jack Forster.
© Andy Davey

James Simpson-Daniel.
© Andy Davey

Lesley Vainikolo.
© Andy Davey

Luke Narraway.
© Andy Davey

Marco Bortolami.
© Andy Davey

Mark Foster.
© Andy Davey

Matthew J.
Watkins.
© Andy Davey

Mike Tindall.
© Andy Davey

Nick Wood.
© Andy Davey

Olivier Azam.
© Andy Davey

Olly Barkley.
© Andy Davey

Olly Morgan.
© Andy Davey

Peter Buxton.
© Andy Davey

Rory Lawson.
© Andy Davey

Ryan Lamb.
© Andy Davey

Will James.
© Andy Davey

Willie Walker.
© Andy Davey

FORST OF DEAN VISITORS

There have been four Forest of Dean clubs that have played at Kingsholm. They are Lydney, Forest of Dean combination, Cinderford and Bream.

THE FIRST

The first team to visit Kingsholm after the Great War of 1914-1918 was Lydney in the 1919-20 season. George Holford was the Club Captain and the visitors suffered a 13 points to three setback.

CAPTAIN OF FRANCE

Philippe St Andre was a player with the Club when he captained France against Argentine, Italy, Romania and South Africa (twice) in 1997.

NATIONAL CUP WINNERS – F

John Fidler	1978
Paul Ford	1982
Terry Fanolua	2003
Rob Fidler	2003
James Forrester	2003

A FIJIAN AT KINGSHOLM

The first Fijian International Rugby player to play for Gloucester Rugby Club was Akapusi Qera in the 2007-08 season. He made his Guinness League debut as a replacement versus Sale Sharks on 13 October in a 31 points to twelve victory.

FORWARD CAPTAIN – UNTIL!

All the captains of the Club since the advent of professional Rugby Union had been forwards! Mike Tindall broke that sequence with his appointment as Captain for the 2008/09 season.

FOREIGN COACH

The Club's first foreign coach was former French captain Philippe St Andre.

FOES!

French XV, First Glosters, Forest of Dean Combination, French Universities and Fylde.

FORSTER TO THE FRONT

Gloucester prop forward, Jack Forster, appeared as a 60th minute replacement for England Saxons in their 17 points to thirteen win over New Zealand Maoris at Twickenham on 2nd June 2007 in the Churchill Cup Final. Olly Barkley, then of Bath R.F.C. appeared at fly half throughout the course of the match.

HELPING THE FRENCH

Yorkshire born Dave Ellis who was the Gloucester Rugby Club defence coach has been the France International defence coach for several seasons. Dave is now in a similar position with London Irish. Still part of the national coaching team, he joined Le Bleu's staff in 2001.

FANTASTIC

Mark Mapletoft contributed 54.10% of Gloucester's points in the 1997-98 season with 277 points.

FIRST SEASON

In the first season of the Cheltenham and Gloucester Cup in the 1997-98 season, Gloucester R.F.C. defeated Fylde 88-0 (Home), Wakefield 48-7 (Home), lost to Northampton 30-5 (Away) and defeated West Hartlepool 35-13 (Away) in Pool A matches. The final table read:

	P	W	D	L	F	A	Pts
Gloucester	4	3	0	1	176	50	6
Northampton	4	3	0	1	123	39	6
Wakefield	4	3	0	1	75	95	6
West Hartlepool	4	2	0	2	78	107	2
Fylde	4	0	0	4	21	182	0

In the quarter final Richmond were defeated at Kingsholm 39-27. In the semi-final it was Leicester 15, Gloucester 55 at Welford Road. In the final at Northampton versus Bedford it was a 33-25 victory to take the trophy.

The Gloucester team was:

A. Lumsden; R. Jewell, T. Fanolua, R. Tombs, P. St Andre; M. Mapletoft L. Beck; T. Woodman, N. McCarthy, A. Deacon, R. Ward, D. Sims, S. Ojomoh, P. Glanville and S. Devereaux.

CAPTAINS – F

One player who has been appointed Club Captain with their surname commencing with the letter 'F' was:

Peter Ford (1955-56), (1956-57), (1957-58), (1959-60), (1960-61).

OFF TO FRANCE IN 1911

The Kingsholm club, then known as the 'City', made the trip to Toulouse on 27th February 1911. The 'City' asked for a guarantee of £150 from the French club conditioned that the 'City' were at full strength. The team travelled to London on the 25th after a match at Abertillery, crossed to Paris where they stayed on Sunday night. On Monday they travelled to Toulouse, played the match on the Tuesday, returned to Paris on the Wednesday and were back in Gloucester on Thursday. The 28th (Shrove Tuesday) was a holiday in France.

FORTRESS KINGSHOLM

SEASONS	PLAYED	WON	DREW	LOST	POINTS FOR	POINTS AGAINST
1891-92	22	18	2	2	251	38
1892-93	18	10	1	7	115	52
1893-94	18	13	1	4	181	80
1894-95	17	10	1	6	166	86
1895-96	17	6	4	7	110	98
1896-97	18	13	2	3	175	45
1897-98	19	14	4	1	206	32
1898-99	21	18	0	3	217	77
1899-00	17	13	1	3	237	43
1900-01	20	17	2	1	346	23
1901-02	22	16	2	4	404	69
1902-03	17	12	0	5	261	70
1903-04	19	12	0	7	270	112
1904-05	22	18	2	2	387	52
1905-06	24	20	1	3	578	107
1906-07	19	15	0	4	286	75
1907-08	22	20	0	2	276	109
1908-09	21	13	4	4	282	119
1909-10	23	20	1	2	319	82
1910-11	20	16	1	3	371	68
1911-12	21	16	3	2	261	94
1912-13	23	15	3	5	279	92
1913-14	21	18	1	2	266	54
NO FIXTURES DURING FIRST WORLD WAR						
1919-20	18	13	1	4	225	95
1920-21	21	19	2	0	295	92
1921-22	23	18	2	3	372	87
1922-23	24	20	2	2	335	104
1923-24	21	17	1	3	323	136
1924-25	24	17	1	6	323	162
1925-26	22	14	1	7	300	161
1926-27	26	21	0	5	325	213
1927-28	27	19	0	8	365	164
1928-29	21	15	1	5	324	130
1929-30	21	14	5	2	254	117
1930-31	20	12	6	2	214	116
1931-32	24	18	1	5	241	146

1932-33	21	17	0	4	318	136
1933-34	22	19	1	2	383	93
1934-35	24	20	0	4	462	132
1935-36	21	15	2	4	288	130
1936-37	23	14	1	8	270	176
1937-38	22	20	0	2	286	108
1938-39	20	13	2	5	178	122
1939-40	17	10	5	2	275	149

NO FIXTURES DURING SECOND WORLD WAR

1945-46	21	16	2	3	352	132
1946-47	19	16	0	3	307	133
1947-48	20	18	0	2	350	109
1948-49	24	18	3	3	312	116
1949-50	23	12	5	6	185	111
1950-51	29	19	4	6	302	130
1951-52	26	21	2	3	406	158
1952-53	25	19	2	4	314	164
1953-54	26	22	0	4	297	164
1954-55	25	14	3	8	252	206
1955-56	22	11	3	8	251	159
1956-57	26	13	5	8	249	147
1957-58	26	18	1	7	247	175
1958-59	27	12	3	12	285	279
1959-60	21	16	1	4	307	190
1960-61	31	15	6	10	314	272
1961-62	22	15	1	6	316	185
1962-63	22	15	2	5	336	144
1963-64	24	16	1	7	298	197
1964-65	25	22	0	3	430	179
1965-66	27	15	3	9	312	242
1966-67	32	20	2	10	345	272
1967-68	30	14	5	11	351	288
1968-69	33	23	2	8	658	281
1969-70	33	22	1	10	522	241
1970-71	30	27	2	1	595	191
1971-72	23	22	1	0	489	170
1972-73	28	21	2	5	623	266
1973-74	29	24	2	3	661	282
1974-75	30	27	0	3	747	270
1975-76	28	20	2	6	667	285
1976-77	31	23	2	6	799	261
1977-78	26	24	0	2	671	200

1978-79	30	23	2	5	552	252
1979-80	28	21	2	5	627	242
1980-81	24	22	0	2	530	216
1981-82	28	28	0	0	720	162
1982-83	27	19	3	5	518	246
1983-84	31	22	1	8	658	372
1984-85	28	24	1	3	775	272
1985-86	23	19	0	4	581	184
1986-87	24	17	0	7	558	272
1987-88	27	23	0	4	708	287
1988-89	22	20	0	2	609	203
1989-90	28	22	1	5	774	327
1990-91	27	23	0	4	856	231
1991-92	21	17	0	4	506	236
1992-93	20	17	0	3	509	213
1993-94	23	16	1	6	574	270
1994-95	22	11	0	11	615	304
1995-96	17	12	0	5	448	279
1996-97	23	15	1	7	669	379
1997-98	18	15	0	3	597	300
1998-99	17	12	1	4	466	334
1999-00	16	14	0	2	487	260
2000-01	16	10	1	5	397	288
2001-02	16	15	0	1	764	238
2002-03	16	16	0	0	560	233
2003-04	16	14	0	2	476	261
2004-05	17	10	0	7	369	329
2005-06	17	13	0	4	562	267
2006-07	17	16	0	1	539	298
2007-08	16	13	1	2	420	252
2008-09	16	13	0	3	409	279

THE FINISHING LINE

Since the game of Rugby Union adopted professionalism the Club have finished in the following League positions each season:

1996-97 – 7th, 1997-98 – 7th, 1998-99 – 10th, 1999-2000 – 3rd, 2000-2001-8th, 2001-2002 – 3rd, 2002-2003 – 1st, 2003-2004 – 4th, 2004-2005 – 6th, 2005-2006 – 5th, 2006-2007 – 1st, 2007-2008 – 1st. 2008-2009 – 6th.

FRENCH INFLUENCE

Closely following the appointment of Philippe St Andre as the Club's Director of Coaching an influx of French club players arrived at Kingsholm, including his brother Raphael. Others who followed were:

D. Djoudi, L. Sanchez, O. Azam, G. Gregoire, F. Schisano, K. Sewabu, P. Calleit, P. Collezo, F. Pucciariello, L. Mercier, C. Stoica, D. Yachvili, C. Califano and S. Simon.

FULL BACKS

Gloucester Rugby Club has provided no fewer than 8 full backs that have represented England:

I. Balshaw, H. Boughton, P. E. Butler, W. G. Hook, G. W. Parker, D. Rutherford, O. Morgan and A. E. Wood.

JAMES FORRESTER

Made one of the most unusual debuts for England. James made his bow on the field of play for just two minutes! He came onto the field of play as a blood replacement for Wasps Joe Worsley at the Millennium Stadium, Cardiff on 5th February 2005 versus Wales.

FIRST GATE RECEIPTS

In the 1897-88 season when Blackheath visited Kingsholm a crowd of 5,000 spectators paid £107 to watch the match. The highest receipts to date surpassing the £160 set when Cardiff visited the previous season.

JAMES FORRESTER

James Forrester scored a hat trick of tries in successive seasons versus Bristol. He did so in a Zurich League match in 2001 and in a Powergen Cup trio in 2002. He also recorded a hat trick of tries in a European Cup match with Caerphilly in 2001. His career was sadly cut short when he suffered a serious knee injury at Ashton Gate, Bristol in a re-arranged home fixture as Kingsholm was declared unusable due to construction work on a new stand.

FINAL DAY

Could the 'Cherry and Whites', maintain form until the final day of the season? Statistics show that over the 107 year period since the Club began playing at Kingsholm the 'Cherry and Whites' have won 61 matches on the final day, drawn 6 and lost 38, so they are in credit. Well before the professional era the Club recorded three last day of the season wins in away matches at Bath! They did so in 1904/05 (11-6), 1913/14 (10-3), 1920/21 (11-6). Capital letters denote Home Match.

1891-92	PENARTH	Won	15-0
1892-93	STROUD	Lost	2-5
1893-94	CASTLEFORD	Won	16-8
1894-95	WIGAN	Won	5-0
1895-96	PENARTH	Lost	3-5
1896-97	BROUGHTON	Won	15-3
1897-98	Penarth	Drew	6-6
1898-99	Leicester	Lost	4-6
1899-1900	OLD CROCKS	Won	19-6

1900-01	Northampton	Won	16-10
1901-02	SWANSEA	Lost	0-9
1902-03	Penarth	Won	20-0
1903-04	Northampton	Won	16-0
1904-05	Bath	Won	11-6
1905-06	BATH	Won	3-0
1906-07	Lydney	Won	8-0
1907-08	BRISTOL	Won	14-3
1908-09	Lydney	Won	8-0
1909-10	LYDNEY	Won	18-0

1910-11	Llanelli	Lost	3-6
1911-12	Devonport Albion	Lost	3-7
1912-13	Cinderford	Drew	0-0
1913-14	Bath	Won	10-3
1919-20	Abertillery	Lost	3-9

1920-21	Bath	Won	8-0
1921-22	Cross Keys	Lost	3-12
1922-23	Cross Keys	Lost	5-9
1923-24	Lydney	Won	15-5
1924-25	Sidmouth	Won	12-0

1925-26	Lydney	Lost	3-5
1926-27	Cinderford	Lost	3-11
1927-28	BATH	Lost	8-10
1928-29	Lydney	Lost	3-6
1929-30	Lydney	Lost	9-12
1930-31	Harlequins	Won	13-10
1931-32	Bath	Lost	3-8
1932-33	HALIFAX	Won	18-5
1933-34	Lydney	Lost	0-8

1934-35	Lydney	Lost	4-16
1935-36	Bristol	Lost	0-13
1936-37	BEDFORD	Lost	6-9
1937-38	Lydney	Won	27-6
1938-39	Harlequins	Lost	3-6
1939-40	SOMERSET POLICE	Won	22-9
1945-46	LONDON HOSPITALS	Won	26-8
1946-47	Bath	Lost	3-8
1947-48	Cardiff	Lost	3-33

1948-49	Teignmouth	Won	9-5
1949-50	Devonport Services	Won	6-3
1950-51	COVENTRY	Won	14-0
1951-52	Teignmouth	Won	9-3
1952-53	Teignmouth	Lost	6-13
1953-54	DEVONPORT SERVICES	Won	26-18
1954-55	EXETER	Won	16-3
1955-56	Teignmouth	Lost	3-5
1956-57	Weston-Super-Mare	Won	6-3

1957-58	Weston-Super-Mare	Drew	3-3
1958-59	Taunton	Won	9-3
1959-60	Devonport Services	Won	30-11
1960-61	Llanelli	Drew	11-11
1961-62	TEIGNMOUTH	Won	20-3
1962-63	PRESIDENTS XV	Drew	14-14
1963-64	STROUD	Won	21-3
1964-65	STROUD	Won	31-8
1965-66	FRENCH UNIVERSITIES	Lost	0-17

1966-67	NEWBRIDGE	Won	14-11
1967-68	Exeter	Lost	11-19
1968-69	EXETER	Won	37-3
1969-70	LIVERPOOL	Lost	16-20
1970-71	EXETER	Won	35-12
1971-72	Moseley	Won	17-6
1972-73	Camborne	Won	70-9
1973-74	Camborne	Won	19-13
1974-75	Northern	Won	14-9

1975-76	Sale	Won	13-3
1976-77	PLYMOUTH ALBION	Won	42-0
1977-78	EXETER	Won	12-0
1978-79	Exeter	Won	23-9
1979-80	EXETER	Won	36-12
1980-81	Exeter	Lost	11-22
1981-82	Moseley	Drew	12-12
1982-83	Waterloo	Won	10-6
1983-84	EXETER	Won	58-9

1984-85	EXETER	Won	59-9
1985-86	Bath	Lost	9-22
1986-87	Exeter	Won	44-12
1987-88	Llanelli	Lost	12-60
1988-89	Lydney	Lost	0-10

1989-90	Bath	Lost	6-48
1990-91	HARLEQUINS	Won	36-19
1991-92	Vancouver(Canada)	Won	23-0
1992-93	HARLEQUINS	Won	25-5

1993-94	Harlequins	Lost	20-38
1994-95	Harlequins	Lost	17-24
1995-96	Saracens	Won	17-10
1996-97	Northampton	Won	27-25
1997-98	Northampton	Won	24-22
1998-99	Northampton	Won	43-41
1999-2000	London Irish	Won	42-40
2000-01	Wasps	Lost	6-18
2001-02	Bristol	Won	28-23

2002-03	Wasps	Lost	3-39
2003-04	Sale	Won	44-35
2004-05	Saracens	Lost	16-24
2005-06	London Irish	Won	36-34
2006-07	Bristol	Won	35-13
2007-08	BATH	Won	8-6
2008-09	Wasps	Lost	3-34

FIRST

It was not only the first match of the season on 5th September 1992 at Kingsholm, but it was also the last visit of a famous old London Club to Kingsholm. We were also entertaining the first Rugby Union Club to be formed. Of course the wiseacres will state that there was rugby before Blackheath but generally the game in its early days was played in schools and colleges.

The very first match we had played against Blackheath was on Saturday 8th October 1898. The visitors arrived with only fourteen players and Gloucester let them borrow the free scoring Charles 'Wacker' Smith. Blackheath were victorious by 8 points to five. The gate receipts were £107, this sum was the highest receipts to date. The previous highest was set in the previous season when an attendance of 5,000 witnessed Cardiff return over the border with a 10-0 score-line in their favour. The receipts from that match were £100.

The 'Cherry and Whites' complete record versus Blackheath was:

	Played	Won	Drew	Lost	Points For	Points Against
Home	16	13	0	3	238	80
Away	7	6	0	1	95	55
Overall	22	18	0	4	333	135

Glo'ster stroll to drab derby win

GLOUCESTER triumphed as expected against their struggling neighbours at Kingsholm in a match as drab as the November weather.

A sparse crowd came to watch a stylish massacre but instead witnessed an uneven clash between two old rivals — one of whom seemed content simply to avoid a drubbing while the other lacked the cutting edge to administer one.

Two tries from the busy Marcus Hannaford and one each from flanker Dave Spencer and winger Nick Price, plus eleven points from the boot of Nick Marment, saw Gloucester home but the scores were mere punctuations in a forgettable encounter.

Cheltenham have won just once this season and have not beaten the Cherry and Whites this decade. They defended well and the pack coped manfully against unrelenting Gloucester pressure — but they were devoid of ideas in attack and never threatened the home try line.

Bright spots for Gloucester were the form of Hannaford, who shone out like a beacon

**Gloucester 27pts
Cheltenham 3**

By Tony Marcovecchio

before leaving the game early after a knock, and a good display by outside half John Roberts.

Making the most of a rare chance at first team level, Roberts showed flair and confidence in orchestrating attacking moves which were liable to end in dropped passes or frustrating pile-ups elsewhere.

The match also marked the debut of Longlevens prop forward Andy Deacon.

Launched

Fullback Marment launched the Gloucester effort with three successful penalties in the first 15 minutes, a John Little penalty for the visitors keeping them in touch.

The remainder of the first half produced no more than Hannaford's first try, the scrum half plunging over in the corner after a back row inspired break. Marment missed the conversion.

Within minutes of the restart Hannaford burrowed through the back legs of his scrummage for a second try and midway through the half Spencer crossed for a tap penalty try which again went unconverted.

The cheers which greeted Price's finalising try were more ironic than celebratory, and Marment's first successful conversion heralded a final whistle warmly welcomed by the Kingsholm patrons.

Gloucester: N. Marment; N. Price, D. Cummings, S. Davies, J. Breeze; J. Roberts, M. Hannaford (capt.); R. Phillips, K. White, A. Deacon, K. Hopson, N. Scrivens, D. Spencer, A. Stanley, L. Cummins. Replacement: L. Gardner for Hannaford.

Cheltenham: M. Roberts; C. White, J. Bacon, P. Cooper, A. Henessey; M. Hawling, J. Little (capt.); N. Kent, P. Sargison, P. Holmyard, M. Roberts, G. Cornish, P. Lodge, J. Morris, K. Jeavons. Replacement: N. Townsend for M. Roberts.

MAN OF MATCH

Marcus Hannaford, a busy display highlighted by two tries.

G

GRANDSTAND

The first grandstand erected at Kingsholm was erected in 1926 at a cost of £2,500.

GUTTED

The grandstand caught fire on 9th September 1933 at midday, destroying the 1,750 seating stand and threatening nearby Bertram Mills Circus which was situated behind the grandstand.

NEW GRANDSTAND

The grandstand was rebuilt and financed by the Club's insurers. The new grandstand had 7,000 seats. It was built in just nine weeks and opened for the Gloucestershire versus Somerset County Championship match on Saturday 11th November 1933.

EXTENDED GRANDSTAND

The main grandstand was extended in 1954.

GATE RECEIPTS

The first match where gate receipts were taken was at the Spa when the 'Flamingoes', a London invitation team was brought to play Gloucester Football Club on February 12th 1870 by the Club's former captain Francis Hartley.

GENEROSITY

Gloucester Football Club, as they were known in 1892, donated a sum of £6.2s.11d to local clubs to be used when they required their players, if the Club needed to replace injured players.

CASTLE GRIM

It was in 1891 that Gloucester Athletic and Football Ground Company Ltd was formed to secure the Kingsholm site. It was actually known as the 'Castle Grim Estate'. It was bought for £4,000 by mortgage and capital which was raised by a share issue. There were 2,805 one pound shares.

GYMNASIUM

In 1905 the new gymnasium was opened. It was designed by a local architect, Harold A. Dancey.

GROUNDS

Before Gloucester Rugby Club settled on residing at Kingsholm, they also considered playing at Theresa Street and Sheephouse Lane which is today known as Tuffley Avenue. The land at Tuffley Avenue eventually became the home of Old Cryptians R.F.C. and Widden Old Boys. The Tuffley Avenue site was the least expensive but was considered too far from the City centre.

Eventually Castle Grim owned by Mr A. V. Hatton was chosen. This gentleman had only just purchased the Castle Grim estate from the Church commissioners.

GROUND SWELL

In 1892 the Club had 1,100 members.

GLOUCESTER AN ORIGINAL

Gloucester Rugby Club was one of the member clubs when the formation of the County Football Union was formed on 11th November 1891 at the Spread

Eagle Hotel, Gloucester. The others were Clifton, Stroud, Royal Agricultural College, Bristol, Cheltenham, Lydney, Sharpness, Dursley and Gordon Wanderers.

WHAT A GENT

'Dai' Gent who joined Gloucester when at St Paul's Trinity College, Cheltenham became a schoolmaster in the City, later in Eastbourne and eventually became a rugby correspondent of a London newspaper.

'G' IN TRIO

Three players with their surnames beginning with the letter 'G' have played for England: David 'Dai' Gent, Andy Gomarsall and Philip Greening.

GROUND SETTERS

Two Gloucester players have played for England in an unchanged England team. They are Don Rutherford who was then playing for Percy Park and Mike Teague. England used the same 15 players for four consecutive matches. England have never been unchanged for five matches!

GONE MISSING

Former Gloucester scrum half Andy Gomarsall missed 73 of England's matches following his debut on 23rd November 1996 until he re-appeared for his country again.

NATIONAL CUP WINNERS – G

John Gadd   1982
Marcel Garvey   2003
Andy Gomarsall   2003

GENT A WINNER

'Dai' Gent led Gloucestershire to their first County Championship win in 1910.'Dai' captained the team to a 23 points to nil victory over Yorkshire at Kingsholm. There were seven Gloucester R.F.C. players in that team. 'Dai' , born in Wales, was capped by England.

GRANDSTAND BUILDERS

Following the original Grandstand being destroyed by fire, the 1933 rebuilt version was constructed by Messrs. W. Jones of Gloucester and Davis Brothers & Co. Ltd. of Wolverhampton.

The original stand was erected in 1926 at a cost of £2,900 and measured 180 feet by 40 feet.

GLOUCESTER FIRST

The first Gloucester R.F.C. team to play under floodlights at Kingsholm that faced the Bosuns on 5th November 1967 was:

D. Rutherford, N. Foice, R. G. Pitt, J. A. Bayliss, J. Groves; J. T. Hopson, M. H. Booth, J. L. Fowke, M. J. Nicholls, M. A. Burton, A. Brinn, J. S. Jarrett, G. G. White, D. W. Owen, R. Smith.

CAPTAIN 'G'

Players with their surname commencing with the letter 'G' who have been appointed Club Captain are:

'Dai' Gent   1906-07
Peter Glanville   1997-98

GENT FOR CORNWALL

'Dai Gent' the Llandovey born scrum half who represented England in five International matches also represented the County of Cornwall at cricket.

GOMMAR'S GRAND SLAM

Andy Gomarsall who attended Bedford School led England's School 18 group in 1992 to their first Grand Slam for eleven years. England defeated Wales 18-3, Ireland 15-9, Scotland 28-0 and France 12-9. The former Gloucester Rugby scrum half scored two tries for England on his debut at senior level versus Italy in 1996.

GARVEY SOON ON THE MARK

Former Gloucester wing three-quarter Marcel Garvey scored a hat trick of tries in only his second Zurich Premiership match versus Bristol at Kingsholm on 21st September 2002.

GLOUCESTERSHIRE

When Gloucester R.F.C. travelled to Southend to face the Warners Bridge Club in the 3rd Round of the John Players Cup on 24th January 1981, they were the second team from Gloucestershire to face the Essex club in that season's tournament. Stroud R.F.C. had entertained Southend in the 2nd Round on 6th December, losing a narrow encounter at Fromehall Park by 16 points to thirteen.

GRADUATION!

Gloucester Rugby Football Club players who have played for England at Schoolboy level and gained senior caps include the following:

Tom Voyce, Harold Boughton, Peter Kingston, Chris Williams, Steve Ojomoh, R.Hillier, Phil Greening, Mark Mapletoft, Neil McCarthy, Trevor Woodman, Mike Tindall, Iain Balshaw, James Simpson-Daniel, Andy Gomarsall and Peter Richards.

GUILTY MY LORD!

'The Shewell Case' brought Gloucester Rugby Football Club into disrepute. Twickenham took action in 1880 against clubs offering filthy lucre to players.

The Club's roll of players who have turned out for the first XV include one W. Shewell who made just one appearance. He played for the Club on

30th December 1893 at wing three-quarter in an away match at Newport. An away loss by 26 points without reply saw the Welsh team sweep Gloucester aside. At the time W. Shewell played for nearby Stroud R.F.C. They were not amused. The case went via the Gloucestershire R.F.U. to the Rugby Football Union. The charge was 'offering him inducements to throw in his lot with Gloucester'.

The Count Union levied the Club a fine of £10 with the money being donated to the Gloucester District Nursing Society. The Club lodged £50 in an appeal to the Rugby Football Union. A committee was set up to investigate the matter, the resolution passed: 'That the Gloucester Football Club and ground be suspended from playing football for the remainder of the season and that all the expenses of this enquiry be paid by Gloucester Football Club'.

Bristol offered an 'extra' fixture at Kingsholm in sympathy, this was the Fenners XV won by Gloucester and played on Saturday 21st April 1894. The Enquiry Committee deemed the County return the fine of £10.

ONE OF 12

Gloucester Rugby Club was one of twelve clubs that formed the inaugural Courage League One in 1987. The other clubs were: Bath, Bristol, Coventry, Harlequins, Leicester, Moseley, Nottingham, Orrell, Sale, Wasps and Waterloo.

GLOBAL A-Z

From Australia to Canada the 'Cherry and Whites' have fielded players from all over the world. Gloucester players have represented a total of 16 countries during their time with the Club. Until the age of professional Rugby Union players traditionally hailed from one of the five countries of the British Isles. The following players were born in the country named although they may have represented other nations in International matches.

Argentina	–	Diego Albanese, Carlos Nieto, Frederico Pucciariello
Australia	–	Jason Little, Jeremy Paul, Duncan McRae
Canada	–	Doug Lougheed
France	–	Philippe St Andre, Raphael St Andre, Olivier Azam, Patrice Collazo, Christian Califano, Ludovic Mercier, Frank Schisano, Serge Simon, Stephane Sanchez, Patrice Calleit, Noel Curnier, Dimitri Yachvili, D. Djoudi
Germany	–	Richard Ward, Brian Johnson

Italy	–	Marco Bortolami
Nigeria	–	Steve Ojomoh
Romania	–	Christian Stoica
Samoa	–	Junior Paramore, Terry Fanolua
Tonga	–	Lesley Vainikolo
South Africa	–	Jake Boer, Thinus Delport, D. DuPreez, R. Vande Berg, Quentin Davids, C. Bezuidenhout
Scotland	–	Donald Chrichton-Miller, Alastair Dickinson, Rory Lawson, Alistair Strokosch, Chris Paterson, Steve Brotherstone, Scott Lawson, David Young
Fiji	–	Apo Satala, Akapusi Qera
New Zealand	–	Ian Jones, Elton Moncreiff, H. J. Mynett, D. McGregor, C. Seeling, Nathan Mauger, Martin Kimber, Henry Paul, Andrew Gibbs, Chris Yates, Richard Tombs, Simon Mannix, Greg Somerville, Carlos Spencer, Willie Walker
Wales	–	Danny Evans, John Gwilliam, Willie Jones, Gareth Delve, Gareth Cooper Will James, Tony Lewis, Kingsley Jones, Byron Hayward, Mefin Davies, Gary Powell, James Merriman
Morrocco	–	Gregoire

GLOUCESTERSHIRE XV

In May and June of 1976 Gloucestershire made their first overseas tour which was a seven match one of Rhodesia and South Africa. Among the Gloucester R.F.C. players included were: Peter Butler, Peter Kingston, Bob Clewes, Chris Williams, Richard Mogg, John Fidler, Mike Burton, John Watkins and Brian Vine.

GOOD CAUSE

Gloucester Rugby Club and England centre three quarter Mike Tindall won the final of ITV's All-Star Poker Challenge earning £25,000 for the Parkinson's disease Charity in 2006.

H

HUDSON-RECORDS

Former England International wing three-quarter Arthur Hudson holds the Club record for most tries in a season – 41 scored in the 1905-06 season. The same player also holds the Club record for most tries in a career at Kingsholm – 236.

When Arthur Hudson retired from playing duties he served the Club as Secretary for 35 years combining the duties of Treasurer and Fixture Secretary.

HEINEKEN GLORY, ALMOST!

The Club reached the semi-final of the Heineken Europe Cup in the 2000-2001 season losing by 19 points to 15 to Leicester on 21st April 2001 at Vicarage Road, Watford. A match day programme cost £2.50.

MR HILL

The first match played at Kingsholm between Gloucester R.F.C. and Burton-on-Trent R.F.C. was refereed by Mr Rowland Hill.

HASTINGS ON THE MARK

George Hastings, the former Gloucester Rugby Football Club's prop forward scored a try for England in a match that marked England's 250th International match at Lansdowne Road, Dublin on 12th February 1955. The match was a draw six points apiece.

FOUR AND MORE

The phenomenal Arthur Hudson scored four tries in an International match between England and France on 22nd March 1906 in Paris. It was the first match played between the two countries.

Arthur Hudson is one of eight England International players to have recorded a try in every 80 minutes he played. Arthur scored 9 tries in his eight International appearances. In 640 minutes of playing time averaging 71.1 minutes per try.

HAT TRICK HERO

Arthur Hudson is one of 25 players who have recorded a hat-trick of tries for England.

HILL THE FIRST

In September 1955 Richard Hill was appointed as Director of Rugby. Hill had previously played at scrum half for Gloucester's great South West rivals Bath R.F.C.

HAT TRICKS – LEAGUE

There have been 9 hat-tricks with three tries or more in League fixtures since the advent of professionalism. They have been as follows:

1996-97 Mike Lloyd (3) Versus West Hartlepool – 18th January 1997 (Home)
1998-99 Chris Catling (3) Versus Newcastle – 17th October 1998 (Home)
1999-00 Elton Moncreiff (4) Versus Bedford – 6th May 1999 (Home)
2000-01 Frank Schisano (3) Versus Rotherham – 2nd September 2000 (Away)
2001-02 James Simpson-Daniel (3) Versus Bath – 4th May 2002 (Home)
2002-03 Marcel Garvey (3) Versus Bristol – 21st September 2002 (Home)
2002-03 James Forrester (3) Versus Bristol – 16th March 2003 (Away)
2007-08 Lesley Vainikolo (5) Versus Leeds – 16TH September 2007 (Away)
2007-08 Akapusi Quera (3) Versus Leeds – 19th April 2008 (Home)

EUROPEAN COMPETITION

In European Competitions since the 1996-97 season eight hat-tricks have been recorded:

1996-97	Mark Mapletoft (4) versus West Hartlepool – 12th October 1996 European Conference (Home)
1997-98	Peter Glanville (3) versus Padova – 7th September 1997 European Conference (Home)
2000-01	Tom Beim (5) versus Roma – 14th October 2000 Heineken Cup (Home)
2001-02	James Forrester (3) versus Caerphilly – 27th October 2001 European Shield
2001-02	Daren O'leary (5) versus Gran Parma – 5th January 2002 European Shield (Home)
2002-03	Terry Fanolua (3) versus Viadana – 18th October 2002 Heineken Cup (Away)
2002-03	James Simpson-Daniel (3) versus Viadana – 18th October 2002 Heineken Cup (Away)
2005-06	James Simpson-Daniel (4) versus Bucceresti – 29th October 2005 European Challenge Cup (Home)

Only one hat-trick has been recorded in domestic competition:

2001-02	James Forrester (3) versus Bristol – 16th December 2001 Powergen Cup (Away)

ALL THE 'H's

Seven players with their surname commencing with the letter H have played for England: Charles Hall, George Hastings, Andy Hazell, George Holford, Bill Hook, Percy Hordern and Arthur Hudson.

OPPONENTS IN 'H' BLOCK

Opponents have been: Hamilton, Halifax, Harlequins, Harrogate, Hartlepool Old Boys, Hartlepool Rovers, Headingly, Henley Hawks and High Wycombe.

HUDSON IN HARNESS

Arthur Hudson played soccer for City Albion when they used a pitch sited where the existing Kingsholm car park is now situated. Arthur was introduced to the neighbouring Rugby club in 1904. Arthur passed away on Friday 27th July 1973 at the age of 90 in the Club's Centenary Year.

ANOTHER HUDSON

Arthur Hudson's son Gordon scored 4 tries for England in a war time international. He was serving in the Royal Air Force.

HUDSON LEADS THE WAY

A century of try scorers:

Arthur Hudson	236
Peter Ford	146
Charles Smith	137
S. A. Brown	112
R. J. Clewes	111

HASTINGS IN THE 'GRAND'

George Hastings appeared for England versus Scotland at Twickenham on 16 March 1957 when the expression 'grand slam' was used in the Times report. It was regarded as the first time that expression had been used. George also appeared for England versus Australia at Twickenham on 1st February 1958 when the hosts recorded their first post-war victory over a Dominion team by nine points to six.

ALL IN HASTE

When George Hastings was selected by England to make his International debut in January 1956 he made the trip to Cardiff to find the match postponed due to heavy snow. The former Gloucester Rugby Football Club prop forward was one of six new caps to make his debut one week later.

HASTINGS THE FIRST

Gloucester Rugby Club prop forward George Hastings was an ever present in the England International team when they won the Triple Crown Grand Slam and Five Nations Championship in 1957.

HILL IN 400TH INTERNATIONAL

Richard Hill, the former Gloucester Rugby Club coach was a member of the England team that played their 400th International match when they defeated the United States of America in the first ever Rugby World Cup. England triumphing by 34 points to six in Sydney, Australia on 3 June 1987. Richard was then a playing member of Bath R.F.C.

HANDFUL – ALMOST

George Hastings scored a try, a conversion and penalty goal during his 13 caps for England. The only scoring action he missed out on was a dropped goal! The Dursley born prop forward was England's 851st cap.

HALLS THE NAME

There have been 10 players with the name of Hall that have appeared in the Clubs 1st XV. They were:

Albert Hall 1901-1923, B. Hall 1965, C. Hall 1893-1901, E. Hall 1904-1910, G. Hall 1927–1928, George Hall 1897-1901, H. Hall 1903, J. Hall 1908-1919, S. Hall 1973-75, and W. Hall 1908-1911.

POPULAR HUGHES

The surname of Hughes has been popular in the annals of Gloucester R.F.C. no fewer than eight with this name have appeared in the Club's 1st XV. They are:

A. F. Hughes 1891-1895, D. Hughes 1948, E. H. Hughes 1921-1926, H. Hughes 1905, Reverend Mervyn Hughes 1937-11939, W. Hughes 1897-1898, W. Hughes 1912, and W. D. C. Hughes 1938.

CAPTAIN 'H'

Players who have been appointed Club Captain with their surname commencing with the letter 'H' are:

Francis Hartley	1873-1874, 1874-1875, 1875-1876
John Harman	1893-1894, 1894-1895
Arthur Hudson	1908-1909, 1909-1910, 1910-1911, 1911-1912
George Holford	1912-1913, 1919-1920
Alan Holder	1963-1964
George Hudson	1947-1948, 1948-1949, 1949-1950
Bob Hodge	1952-1953
George Hastings	1954-1955
Marcus Hannaford	1987-1988, 1988-1989
Mike Hamlin	1989-1990, 1990-1991

TED HORSFALL

Ted, made 10 appearances for Gloucester in 1945 scoring one try and later gained an England cap whilst playing for Harlequins. Born on 11th August 1917 in Huddersfield he also played for Huddersfield and Bedford before coming to Kingsholm and moving onto Headingley. After leaving Huddersfield he finished his career at Cardiff. When he was awarded the solitary International cap on 15th January 1949 versus Wales in Cardiff he became the 792nd player to represent England. The former Gloucester R.F.C. flanker passed away in 1981 in Bracknell.

HARMONY

Clive Jacobs, Eric Evans and George Hastings made 9 appearances in a front row combination for England.

DAVID HOLLAND

Dave who was born in Gloucester in 1886 and educated at Linden School was capped by England after moving to Devonport Albion. The forward made two International appearances, making his debut on 20th January 1912 versus Wales at Twickenham. Dave who became the 519th player to represent England only made one other appearance for his country. Dave who later moved North to play Rugby League for Oldham made 110 appearances between 1906 and

1909 at Kingsholm scoring 16 tries and one conversion. Dave passed away on 7th March 1945 in Gloucester.

CHARLES ALEXANDER HOOPER

Charles was born in nearby Stonehouse on 6th June 1869. He was educated at Clifton College and played for Cambridge University and after joining Gloucester he left the Club to play for Middlesex Wanderers. The centre three-quarter was capped by England and make his debut on 6th January 1894 versus Wales at Birkenhead Park a match which England won by 24 points to three. Charles was the 264th player to be capped by England and in total was awarded three caps. He played for this Club between 1891 and 1893 making 59 appearances scoring five tries. Charles passed away in Taplow, Buckinghamshire on 16th September 1950.

HALT!

Gordon Hudson appeared as Corporal A. G. Hudson in the Great Britain team that faced the Dominions at Leicester on Saturday 31st March 1945. Gordon was one of eight R.A.F. players in the Great Britain team.

PERCY HORDERN

Percy was one of three former Gloucester Rugby Club players to have played for England on an Easter Monday. Percy did so on 6th April 1931 in a one point defeat by 14-13 at Slade Colombes, Paris against France.

HEINEKEN CUP

The Heineken Cup that the 'Cherry and Whites', constantly strive to obtain is made of seven kilos of solid silver and is 50 centimetres tall.

NATIONAL CUP WINNERS – H

Peter Howell	1978
Andy Hazell	2003

I

ONLY ENGLAND INTERNATIONAL

At the only England International match at senior level staged at Kingsholm on 6th January 1900 there was an attendance of 15,000 spectators versus Wales. The gate receipts were £46 7s 3d. Wales defeated England by 13 points to three. There were thirteen new caps in the England team.

ITALY TO THE FORE

Italian International Captain Marco Bortolami was the 66th appointment as Captain of Gloucester Rugby Club in 2005.

INSURANCES

Insurances for players were raised by member's subscriptions in 1899 following a number of injuries which had resulted in several broken bones.

IN HASTE

For the first International match played at Kingsholm England v Wales new stands were erected to increase the capacity to 28,670. However, there were no players from Gloucester selected and only 15,000 spectators attended.

IMPORTS

The first 'imported' players to appear for the Club came when the visiting New Zealand team of 10th October 1905 stayed on in the City and two of their players appeared for Gloucester. They were H. J. Mynett and D. McGregor.

ALL THE I's

Opponents: International XV, Ireland.

IBBOTSON ON 'GLAWS'

Doug Ibbotson once remarked 'The Holy Writ of Gloucester Rugby Club demands: first that the forwards shall win the ball, second that the forwards shall keep the ball and third, the backs shall buy the beer'.

INSTEAD

Hucclecote born Phil Mathews could so easily have been a 'Cherry and White'; instead the flanker ignored Gloucester and England and instead gained 38 caps for Ireland.

INTERNATIONAL PLAYERS

Gloucester Rugby Club during the season of 2007-2008 had more Internationals on their playing staff than in any previous season.

England:	Anthony Allen, Iain Balshaw, Olly Barkley, Alex Brown, James Forrester, Andy Hazell, Olly Morgan, Luke Narraway, James Simpson-Daniel, Mike Tindall, Andy Titterell, Leon Lloyd and Lesley Vainokola.
France:	Oliver Azam, Christian Califano and Patrice Collazo.
Italy:	Marco Bortolami and Carlos Nieto.
Wales:	Gareth Delve, Gareth Cooper and Will James.
Scotland:	Alasdair Dickinson, Chris Paterson, Rory Lawson and Alasdair Strokosch.
Australia:	Jeremy Paul
Fiji:	Akapusi Qera

ITALIAN INTERNATIONALS

Marco Bortolami and Carlos Nieto were not the first Italian Internationals to play for Gloucester Rugby Club. Christian Stoica preceded them. Christian played in the first six matches of the 2001/2002 season, his only appearances for the Club. He then departed to French Club Castres.

INTERNATIONAL

Gloucester Rugby Football Club supplied four players for the England team that played South Africa in Port Elizabeth in 1984: J. H. Fidler, M. Preedy, S. G. F. Mills and P. J. Blakeway.

INTERNATIONAL XV's

Both England and Ireland sent representative teams to Kingsholm in the 1991/1992 season.

GLOUCESTER R.F.C.'s ENGLAND PLAYERS WHO NEVER APPEARED IN AN INTERNATIONAL IN THIS COUNTRY WHILST WITH THE KINGSHOLM CLUB

Rob Fidler, John Fidler, Dave Sims, Gordon Sargent, Charles (Whacker) Smith, Richard West, Christopher Williams, Scott Benton, Peter Butler, Peter Hordern, Mark Mapletoft, Steve Ojomoh, Malcolm Preedy and Tom Price.

IRISH PHIL!

When Ireland met Gloucester at Kingsholm on Saturday 20th 1991 they were captained by Hucclecote born Phil Matthews.

IN BALANCE

An attendance of 16,000 witnessed the England versus Wales wartime International at Kingsholm on Saturday 15th April and the gate receipts were £2,500. After expenses had been deducted the balance was sent to the Red Cross Fund.

ITALY

Steve Ojomoh-Parma and Tom Beim-Viadana are two England Internationals to have played in Italy's premier league, Steve in 2001-02 and Tom from 2003 to 2005.

INTACT

The team that welcomed Ireland to Kingsholm in 1991 was:

T. Smith; J. Perrins, D. Caskie, S. Morris, N. Marment; N. Matthews, M. Hannaford; P. Jones, J. Hawker, R. Phillips, P. Miles, D. Sims, P. Ashmead, I. Smith (Captain), S. Masters. The replacements were: R. Williams, L. Gardiner, D. Kearsey, A. Deacon, B. Clark, S. Deveraux.

In the 14 points to thirteen victory tries were scored by Jerry Perrins and Simon Morris with Tim Smith adding two penalties.

The Ireland team were:

J. Staples (London Irish); S. Geoghegan (London Irish), B. Mullin (Blackrock), D. Curtis (London Irish), J. Clarke (Dolphin); R. Keyes (Cork Constitution), R. Saunders (London Irish); N. Popplewell (Greystones), S. Smith (Ballymera), D. Fitzgerald (D. L. S. P.), D. Lenihan (Cork Constitution), M. Galway (Shannon), P. Matthews (Wanderers, Captain), G. Hamilton (Ballymena) and B. Robinson (Ballymena).

Replacements: K. Murphy, N. Barry, F. Aherne, T. Kingston, G. Halpin and N. Mannion.

Referee: Matt Bayliss (Gloucestershire Society).

FIRST IRISH VISITING

Gloucester had been playing at Kingsholm for 62 years before a team from Ireland paid a visit. It was in 1955-56 that Dublin Wanderers sent a team. A 12 points to three victory resulted for the hosts. Bective Rangers from Dublin are the only Irish Club to have visited Kingsholm. The other visitors from across the sea have been Irish Wolfhounds, a type of Irish Barbarians team and the Divisional Munster who first visited Kingsholm on Monday 22nd September 1986, the visitors winning 28-16.

INTERNATIONAL VISIT

It was Thursday 19th October 1905. Gloucester R.F.C. took on the might of New Zealand. The first International team to take on the Cherry and Whites. The teams for that midweek fixture were:

GLOUCESTER	NEW ZEALAND
FULLBACK	FULLBACK
L. Vears	G. Gillett
C. Smith	G. W. Smith
F. Hall	R. J. Deans
J. Harrison	W. Wallace
A. Hudson	
HALF BACKS	FIVE-EIGHTS
J. Stephens	J. Hunter
A. Wood	W. Stead
D. R. Gent	HALF BACK
	F. W. Roberts
FORWARDS	FORWARDS
W. Johns (Captain)	F. Glasgow
A. Hawker	W. Glenn
F. Pegler	W. Cunningham
G. Vears	G. Nicholson
B. Parham	J. O'Sullivan
H. Collins	C. Seeting
G. Matthews	W. Johnstone
	D. Gallagher (Wing & Captain)

For this match Gloucester decided to play only seven forwards as they thought the extra half-back would be more useful than a wing forward.

IT'S IN THE FAMILY

James Forrester's grandfather, David Naylor, captained Coventry R.F.C. and also played for Bath. While his father played for Oxford R.F.C. and Oxfordshire. A promising centre half, James had trials for Oxford United at soccer.

J

JACKSON

Walter Jesse Jackson was the first Gloucester born player to represent England. Walter had originally played for Gloucester R.F.C. but left to play for Halifax R.F.C. He made his International debut on 17th March 1894 versus Scotland at Raeburn Place, Edinburgh. Scotland were the victors with two tries 6-0. The match was England's 51st International.

JONES

Two players by the name of Jones have scored a hat trick of dropped goals in a match. W. E. Jones versus Bedford in the 1946/47 season and D. Jones versus Northampton in the 1955/56 season.

LITTLE WILLIE JONES

Willie Jones, the former Glamorgan County cricketer recorded the most drop goals in a season with a total of 17 in the 1946/47 season.

JOHN PLAYER

The John Player Cup Final of 1978 saw Gloucester defeat Leicester in first season of its conception. It was a match where Referee Roger Quittendon awarded 15 penalties against Gloucester!

ONLY JOHN

William Johns is the only player with his surname commencing with the letter 'J' who has appeared for England.

LAST JOHN

William Johns of Gloucester Rugby Football Club played in the last International match to be played at Richmond on 20th March 1909. A match in which England were defeated by eighteen points to eight.

JOHNS IN 100TH

William Johns played in England's 100th International match when they played Wales at Cardiff in the Arms Park on 16 January 1909. Wales were victorious by eight points to nil.

NATIONAL CUP WINNERS

John Jarrett   1972
Richard Jardine   1978
Les Jones   1982

CAPTAIN JONES

'All Blacks' legend, Ian Jones, captained Gloucester Rugby Club in the 2000/01 season.

JUBILEE

The Club's Jubilee Year was celebrated in 1933.

JAMES BY NAME

There have been no fewer than ten players with the surname of James who have appeared for the Club's 1st XV. They are:

A. James 1901-1902, A. James 1937, A. C. James 1891-1893, E. M. James 1927, E. T. James 1898-1900, G. R. James 1924-1938, R. James 1906, R. H. James 1921-1923, Reverend D. James 1945, and W. James 2006-present.

JONES SURPASSES THEM ALL

The surname of Jones has been the most popular surname in the annals of the Club. Those that have appeared in the Club's 1st XV:

A. Jones 1901, B. Jones 1956-1957, D. A. Jones 1954-1958, D. W. Jones 1948-1957, E. Jones 1919, G. Jones 1950-1957, G. F. Jones 1891-1893, G. L. Jones 1906, I. Jones 1948-1950, Ivor Jones 1936, J. Jones 1965, M. C. Jones 1954, N. Jones 1945, P. Jones 1931, R. Jones 1947, R. Jones 1969, R. L. Jones 1973-1975, T. J. Jones 1953-1954, W. Jones 1902-1909, W. Jones 1938, Kingsley Jones 1999-2000, P. Jones, I. Jones 2000-2002 – twenty-three in total.

LETTER 'J'

The following players have captained the Club with their surname commencing with 'J':

William Johns in tandem with George Romans (1904-05), Ray James (1930-1931), Kingsley Jones (1999-2000) and Ian Jones (2000-2001).

JAPANESE AT KINGSHOLM

When the Japanese toured England in 1976 they met Gloucestershire at Kingsholm. A margin of 52 points accrued in defeating the overseas visitors. The County were three stone on average weight heavier in the scrum and three inches taller in the line outs. The County scored 11 tries! Richard Mogg and Richard Jardine scored three tries apiece and Gordon Sargent, Brian Vine and Steve Mills, all of Gloucester R.F.C., were among those who pierced the Japanese defence in front of a 10,000 attendance.

JOHNS MEETS EDGAR MOBBS

When William Johns the former Gloucester R.F.C. lock forward made his debut for England versus Wales on 16th January 1909 he did so alongside Northampton R.F.C.'s wing three quarter Edgar Mobbs.

Edgar, serving in the Army, was killed in action at Zillekete in 1917 in the Great War of 1914-18. Today there is an annual match played at Franklin Gardens, the home of Northampton R.F.C. between East Midlands and the Barbarians for the Edgar Mobbs Memorial Trophy.

JONES – HAND AND FOOT

Former Glamorgan County cricketer, Willie Jones, who joined the Club in the 1945-46 season averaged six points a game for the Club. In three and a half seasons at Kingsholm before his move to Neath he had made 77 appearances and scored 462 points. Of the points total 15 came from five tries – the remainder from his boot!

The members' area at Kingsholm

K

KINGSHOLM ON SERVICE

Kingsholm hosted the Services Internationals between England and Wales. The first on 28th March 1942. This wartime International was won by Wales, 9 points to three. Further matches were staged between the two countries at Kingsholm in 1943, 1944 and 1945.

SPECIAL 'K'

Peter Kingston is the only player with the letter 'K' commencing his surname to have played for England.

KINGSHOLM OUT OF 18

Kingsholm is one of 18 of all England's home grounds. It was host to the International with Wales on 6 January 1900.

KINGSHOLM ON WARFRONT

Kingholm hosted four of the 24 wartime Internationals staged during the Second World War, none of which have ever been listed as capped matches.

OPPONENTS – K

Kent Wanderers.

KING OF ALL

'Kingsholm is the best ground in the country' is how Engineer Commander S. F. Cooper, Secretary of the Rugby Football Union stated in April 1940.

KNOCK OUT

In the 1979/80 season the Club's 1978 John Player Cup side met the Club's 1972 Knock Out Cup team. Despite a hat trick of tries by Richard Mogg for the '78 team, it proved not enough and the '72 team won by a single point in a 28-27 victory.

Saints suffer by half

 Gloucester **40**
Tries: Simpson-Daniel (2), Garvey, Forrester. Cons: Mercier (4). Pens: Mercier (3). Drop goal: Mercier.

 Northampton **22**
Try: Beal. Con: Grayson. Pens: Grayson (5).

Eddie Butler
at Twickenham

LAST YEAR, IN search of a first ever knock-out cup triumph, Northampton came south to Twickenham and got lost on the M1. They never made it. They lost heavily to London Irish. This year they made it. And then, just as mysteriously, they disappeared again.

At the end of a pulsating first half the Saints trailed by just two points. Everything was set up for an equally gripping second period. Except that Gloucester seized total control and Northampton were not to score a single point. In the end Gloucester outscored them four tries to one. Ludovic Mercier finished with 20 points, three penalties and a drop goal, three penalties and four conversions. They even

won the sin-bin count 2-1 with Rob Fidler and Tinus Delport outnumbering Paul Grayson.

Gloucester had no England players to worry about. Nobody arrived at this final exhausted from the grandslam exploits in the Six Nations. James Simpson-Daniel looked so fresh that he was able to go the length of the field in the 82nd minute latching on to a pass from Grayson.

Northampton, on the other hand, had Matt Dawson, Steve Thompson and Ben Cohen, not to mention Steve Williams of Wales and Tom Smith of Scotland. The England contingent all look plain knackered. Which would have been bad enough in itself, except that, for Dawson in particular, fatigue turned into another cup-final nightmare.

The poor old scrum-half, as early as the fourth minute,

threw a pass in his own 22 that eluded its target, Thompson, and Simpson Daniel pounced for his first try. Seventy-nine minutes later it was Dawson's pass, meant for Cohen, that was intercepted by Mercier and that allowed Simpson-Daniel to score his second.

To heap the blame on Dawson's door, as it were, would be unfair. By the time he threw his second pass the Northampton dominated the game was over. And he played a part in a truly gripping opening 40 minutes. This was sparkling rugby in brilliant sunshine, with points coming at regular intervals throughout the half.

Grayson opened proceedings with the first of his five penalties, which not only suggested that Northampton were in no mood to repeat last year's no-show, but also that his record of six penalties in a final was under some threat.

Unfortunately for Northampton, straight from the restart Gloucester stole the lead courtesy of Dawson's pass, seized upon by Gloucester's wing. Now it was Gloucester who were laying out their stall. Their last appearance at Twickenham in a cup final was also a no-show. Back in 1990

they were overwhelmed by Bath. And boy, in the west country, that really hurt.

In the professional age they have expanded their repertoire, and it was one of their Frenchman, Mercier, now of folkloric status, who increased their lead with a sweetly struck drop goal.

Just to show the ebb and flow of the first half, Northampton dominated the next five minutes. Over went two more Grayson penalties into the bin went Fidler for messing about at a ruck, and over went Nick Beal for the Saints' first try. It followed a clean break by Grayson and support from Cohen, and it suggested that the tide might have turned yet again.

And then back the other way. Delport initiated a counterattack, the No8 James Forrester, who has added pace and a whole new vision to the Gloucester back row, sold an outrageous dummy that took him past three defenders. Just as good was his slipped pass to Marcel Garvey and the winger completed the move in style. It was a day when Gloucester's wingers could say that 13 years ago

Grayson kicked his fourth penalty and Northampton were back in the lead. For all of two minutes. Over went Mercier's first penalty. And there was still time for the lead to change hands yet again before the interval, thanks to Grayson's fifth penalty. Who would have thought it would be his last shot at goal? Everything seemed so perfectly set up for an absorbing, evenly matched second half.

It was as if Northampton never came out of the changing room. Within two minutes the two Gloucester wings were going close in one corner. They looked up to see Forrester going over on the other side. It should have been an easy dab down for the No 8, but there was a suggestion that he dropped the ball.

No matter. Gloucester were now in almost-total control of that same ball. Northampton were simply growing more and more ragged. And luck was deserting them. Beal covered back once, only to collide with Ben Cohen and injure himself. After he threw the ball into touch, referee Tony Spreadbury took pity on him and did not penalise him for doing so deliberately.

But the referee was not so kind on Grayson for making an early tackle on Henry Paul Gloucester look a completely different, more fluid side with Paul in the centre and Delport at full-back. Especially when running against 14 players.

When Grayson departed, his side were only five points adrift. When he returned they were trailing by 11. Mercier had kicked two penalties, one a monster from halfway.

As Gloucester's dominance became complete there was still time for Delport to be binned for a push on Dawson and for Dawson to have his second pass intercepted. It was a rotten end to the England scrum-half's day, a sudden reversal of fortune in just six days. Not that Gloucester were thinking of their double completed.

Gloucester: Delport; Garvey, Fanolua, Paul (Todd 74), Simpson-Daniel; Mercier, Gomarsall; Woodman, Azam, Deacon, Eustace, Fidler, Boer (capt), Hazell (Paramore 62), Pearce 74), Forrester.
Northampton: Beal; Reihana, Jorgensen (Hunter 62), Leslie (co-capt), Cohen; Grayson; Dawson; Smith, Thompson, Morris (Stewart 53), Lord, Williams (Fox 76), Connors, Pountney (co-capt), Blowers.
Referee: A Spreadbury (Bath)

L

MATCH RECORDS IN LEAGUE MATCHES

Simon Mannix scored 28 points versus Northampton at Kingsholm on 16th May 1999. Elton Moncrieff scored 4 tries versus Bedford on 15th May 2000 at Kingsholm. The most conversions in a match are held jointly by Simon Mannix and Ludovic Mercier. Simon Mannix kicked 7 conversions versus Bedford on 16th May 2000 at Kingsholm whilst Ludovic Mercier kicked the same total of conversions versus Bath on 4th May 2002 at Kingsholm. Simon Mannix holds the record of most penalties scored in a match when he kicked 9 versus Harlequins at Kingsholm on 23rd September 2000. Ludovic Mercier is the only player to have landed a hat trick of drop goals in a league match when he did so versus Sale on 22nd September 2001.

TEAM RECORDS IN LEAGUE MATCHES IN THE PROFESSIONAL ERA

The most points scored at Kingsholm is 68 versus Bath on 4th March 2002. The most points scored in an away match is 50 versus Leeds on 12th May 2002. The most points conceded at Kingsholm is 45 versus Bath on 21st September 1996. The most points conceded in an away match is 75 versus Harlequins on 31st August 1996.

The most tries scored in a match was 11 versus Sale at Kingsholm on 16th April 1988. This was prior to the game turning professional. The most tries conceded in a match was 11 versus Harlequins on 31st August 1996 and the same total versus Bath on 30th April 1997. The biggest margin of victory was by 56 points when we defeated Bath at Kingsholm on 4th April 2002 by 68 points to twelve.

Our biggest margin of victory in an away match was by 46 points when we defeated Orrell on 16th November 1996 by 49 points to three. The biggest defeat at Kingsholm came on 11th March 2000 when Northampton won by 35 points to eleven securing a winning margin of 24 points. Harlequins collected a 56 point winning margin when they defeated Gloucester at the Stoop by 75 points to nineteen on 31st August 1996.

THE CLUB'S LEADING POINT SCORERS OVER THE LAST TEN SEASONS IN LEAGUE MATCHES HAVE BEEN AS FOLLOWS:

1997-98	Mark Mapletoft	275
1998-99	Mark Mapletoft	198
1999-00	Simon Mannix	282
2000-01	Simon Mannix	187
2001-02	Ludovic Mercier	334
2002-03	Ludovic Mercier	255
2003-04	Henry Paul	206
2004-05	Henry Paul	136
2005-06	Ludovic Mercier	213
2006-07	Willie Walker	159
2007-08	Ryan Lamb	152
2008-09	Olly Barkley	125

LAPPING IT UP

When Llanelli were defeated at Stradey Park in the 1899/1900 season they suffered their first defeat at home for three seasons. Ecstatic Gloucester fans waited until past midnight at the local railway station to welcome home their heroes.

LADIES – NO THANK YOU!

A Ladies Rugby Football Club at Kingsholm was refused by the Club Committee in 1948/49. A request was made by a Miss Violet Pegler. Violet had been taken to watch matches at Kingsholm at the tender age of five. She had played 'touch rugby' when she served in the Army. She had gathered together a team who were coached by a former Gloucester player – Sidney Dangerfield.

At the time the Club President, Dr Alcock, refused to sanction this move stating that it would be 'inadvisable from all points of view'.

LADIES IN STEP

The entire Ladies Committee resigned in 1962 but was eventually replaced by other volunteers.

A LOSS

A loss was incurred in consecutive seasons by Gloucester Rugby Football Club in 1968/69 and 1969/70 with a trading loss of near £1,000 in each season.

'LOCALS'

In 1997 it was reported that Gloucester Rugby Club contained the highest proportion of 'local' players in the Allied Premier League, one with 43% of the first team squad born within 20 miles of the Club.

ALL THE L's

Opponents have been: Launceston, La Rochelle, L'Aquila, Leicester, Lennox, Leeds Tykes, Lewes, Liverpool, Liverpool St Helens, Llanelli, Llanhilleth, Lllysipia, Loughborough College, London Hospitals, London Scottish, London Welsh, Leinster, London Irish and Lydney.

DOUBLE LAWSON

Rory Lawson, the Gloucester Rugby Club scrum half is following in the steps of his father Alan in representing Scotland. Alan scored two tries against England in 1976. Included in the England team that day was Gloucester prop forward Mike Burton.

LAWSON ON THE CHASE

For Rory Lawson to surpass his father Alan's total of International appearances for Scotland he will have to be awarded 16 caps. To the end of the 2007-2008 season he had been awarded twelve.

LEAGUE POSITIONS

Gloucester Rugby Club's League positions since the advent of the professional era have been:

1995-96 – 8th	2002-03 – 1st
1996-97 – 6th	2003-04 – 4th
1997-98 – 7th	2004-05 – 6th
1998-99 – 10th	2005-06 – 5th
1999-00 – 3rd	2006-07 – 1st
2000-01 – 7th	2007-08 – 1st
2001-02 – 3rd	2008-09 – 6th

LEAGUE SPONSERS

Since the innovation of professional Rugby Union there have been four sponsors of the League – Allied Dunbar, Courage, Zurich and Guinness.

LANDMARK

The first player to reach the landmark of 100 League appearances for the Cherry and Whites was former Scotland back row forward Ian Smith. In total the former St Thomas Rich's pupil made 108 League appearances for the Club.

NATIONAL CUP WINNERS

Mike Longstaff   1982

LIONS

Gloucester British Lions:

1899 – F. M. Stout	– to Australia
1924 – A. T. Voyce	– to South Africa
1966 – D. Rutherford	– to New Zealand & Australia
1974 – M. J. Burton	– to South Africa
1980 – P. J. Blakeway	– to South Africa
1983 – J. B. Boyle	– to New Zealand
2001 – P. Vickery	– to Australia

LEWIS

There have been 10 players with the surname of Lewis who have appeared at first team level for Gloucester R.F.C. They are:

A. Lewis (1958), A. W. Lewis (1927-28), Alec Lewis (1908-1919), E. P. Lewis (1954), F. Lewis (1910-12), J. Lewis (1913), Jack Lewis (1897-1901), M. Lewis (1933), P. Lewis (1954-1957), D. Lewis (2007 –)

VIC LEADBETTER

Vic Leadbetter was capped by England on 20th March 1954 versus Scotland at Murrayfield while he was playing for Edinburgh Wanderers. The lock forward only made one other appearance for his country on 10th April 1954 versus France at Stade Colombes. Vic, who was born in Kettering in 1930 was educated at Cambridge University, he moved to Kingsholm in 1956 and left in 1958 making 79 first team appearances scoring 9 tries.

LOCALS

There has always been an abundance of local clubs in Gloucester where Gloucester R.F.C. have been able to recruit players. They include:

Brockworth, Chosen Hill, Coney Hill, Dowty, All Blues, Gloucester Old Boys, Gloucester Police, Gordon League, Hucclecote, I.C.I., Longlevens, Matson, Old Cryptians, Old Richians, Saintbridge, Spartans, Tredworth and Widden.

LEGENDS

It is always debatable as to who are 'Cherry and White' legends. Some are generally recognised others less so. Basically it is a personal opinion. The following would gain general approval:

John G. A'Bear, Tommy Bagwell, John Bayliss, Phil J. Blakeway, Jake Boer, Mickey Booth, Harold Boughton, Alan Brinn, Mike Burton, Peter Butler, Alfred Carpenter, Bob Clewes, Andy Deacon, Charlie Dunn, Terry Fanolua, Peter Ford, John Gadd, Mike Hamlin, George Hastings, Terry Hopson, Arthur Hudson, Dennis Ibbotson, Roy James, David Jones, Ian Jones, Willie Jones, Richard Mogg, Roy 'Digger' Morris, Mike Nicholls, Malcom Preedy, Don

Rutherford, Dave Sims, Charles 'Wacker' Smith, Ian Smith, Dick Smith, Eric Stephens, Roy Sutton, Chris Tanner, Mike Teague, Cyril Thomas, Phil Vickery, Tom Voyce, John Watkins and James Simpson-Daniel.

LEAGUE RECORD 1995-2009

Home

	Season Year	Won	Drew	Lost	Points For	Points Against
Courage League	1995-96	5	0	4	154	149
	1996-97	7	1	3	256	202
Allied Dunbar League	1997-98	9	0	2	303	192
	1998-99	8	1	4	358	284
	1999-00	9	0	2	328	215
	2000-01	7	0	4	231	187
	2001-02	10	0	1	429	189
Zurich League	2002-03	11	0	0	342	159
	2003-04	10	0	1	290	156
	2004-05	6	0	5	228	230
	2005-06	7	0	4	258	197
Guinness Premiership	2006-07	11	0	0	313	185
	2007-08	10	0	1	420	252
	2008-09	9	0	2	278	199

Away

	Season Year	Won	Drew	Lost	Points For	Points Against
Courage League	1995-96	1	0	8	121	221
	1996-97	4	0	7	220	387

Allied Dunbar League	1997-98	2	1	8	207	338
	1998-99	1	0	12	196	359
	1999-00	6	0	5	300	275
Zurich Premiership	2000-01	3	0	8	212	339
	2001-02	4	0	7	263	296
	2002-03	6	2	3	275	237
	2003-04	4	0	7	201	249
	2004-05	4	2	5	218	219
	2005-06	4	1	6	225	188
Guinness Premiership	2006-07	4	2	5	218	219
	2007-08	4	0	7	258	225
	2008-09	3	0	8	157	249

Mercier the sting in a classic tale

BY TIM GLOVER
at Twickenham

Gloucester 40
Tries: Garvey, Forrester; Simpson-Daniel 2
Cons: Mercier 4
Pens: Mercier 3
Drops: Mercier

Northampton 22
Try: Bird
Con: Grayson
Pens: Grayson 5

Half-time: 20-22   Attendance: 75,000

Home James: James Simpson-Daniel runs in Gloucester's first try at Twickenham, much to the disgust of the Northampton hooker Steve Thompson   ROBERT HALLAM

Gloucester may not have much money but are they happy? You bet your life they are. Last night the Cherry and Whites deposited the Powergen Cup in what had been a bare cupboard at Kingsholm, condemning Northampton to yet another defeat in the national knockout competition.

After a fast and furious first half, which Northampton shaded 22-20, Gloucester piled on the agony, coming home like a Grand National winner, by four goals, three penalties and a drop goal to a goal and five penalties.

Both clubs had spirits to exorcise, the Saints after collapsing here to London Irish 12 months ago and Gloucester after an embarrassing defeat by Bath the last time they were in a Twickenham final, 13 years ago. It was Gloucester who possessed the ghostbusters in Ludovic Mercier, James Simpson-Daniel and James Forrester.

Simpson-Daniel twice capitalised on wayward passes from Matt Dawson to help himself to two tries, while the exceptional Forrester made a first-half try for Marcel Garvey and scored one himself in the second. Mercier contributed 20 points and it was his interception from Dawson at the death that sent the Saints to their fourth knock-out final defeat, three of them in the last four seasons.

The lead changed hands six times during an extraordinary first half, at the end of which the players needed water, oxygen and sunblock. Northampton, who were caught cold in last year's final, drew first blood when Paul Grayson landed a penalty following a promising move.

That was in the fourth minute, and a minute later the Saints were cursing their scrum-half Dawson. The man who normally gives the opposition nothing but grief presented Gloucester with a soft score. His pass went nowhere near a Northampton player but instead bounced kindly into the grateful arms of Simpson-Daniel, who could not believe his luck. The wing dashed over, Mercier converted and Gloucester were 7-3 in front.

They had a chance to go further ahead when Andrew Blowers pushed in a late shoulder on Mercier, the stand-off missing the penalty from the half-way line. However, Mercier dropped a goal to make it 10-3 before Northampton responded with 13 points in the space of five minutes. First Grayson missed a penalty but he soon added another when Simpson-Daniel was caught in front of his own posts. As Northampton were about to win quick ball, Rob Fidler fiddled with the flow and not only conceded a penalty but also received a yellow card.

The Saints then went marching in when Grayson sold a dummy in midfield, fooling Simpson-Daniel in the process. He slipped an inside pass to Nick Beal and the full-back sprinted around his opposite number, Thinus Delport, to score at the post. Grayson's conversion transformed the score from 10-3 to 10-16.

Gloucester were not behind for long. Forrester cut a swathe down the Northampton right flank and sold a dummy before spinning a pass inside to Marcel Garvey which resulted in the wing smashing through the last line of defence.

Grayson continued to punish Gloucester and added two more penalties to one by Mercier to give Northampton a 22-20 lead at the interval, which the players desperately needed. It was breathtaking stuff.

Gloucester, of course, wasted no time in regaining the lead. Two minutes after the restart they stretched the Northampton defence to breaking point when Henry Paul threw out a long pass to the right. It was not the best of deliveries, and as it bounced just before reaching Garvey, the wing cleverly flicked it on to Forrester, repaying an earlier compliment, and the No 8 beat Grayson down the right-hand touchline. Mercier made no mistake with the angled conversion.

The Powergen was now with the Cherry and Whites. Northampton suffered a blow when they lost Peter Jorgensen, who suffered a shoulder injury as he attempted to halt a typical charge from Fanolua. When Paul was tackled by Grayson without the ball, it was double jeopardy for the Saints. Not only did Mercier kick the penalty to put clear blue water between the sides, but Grayson was sent to the sin-bin for the tackle.

The Gloucester pack, as they had on two previous occasions this season, were proving the more powerful unit. When they won another penalty, Mercier nailed it from the half-way line. It was not the end of his contribution. In injury time, with Northampton pressing, Mercier intercepted a pass from Dawson and sped 90 yards later Simpson-Daniel touched down for Gloucester's fourth try. The haloes were on Gloucester.

Tom Walkinshaw, the owner of Gloucester, who has seen the demise of his Formula One racing company which in turn has led to cuts at Kingsholm, got his hands on the cup. Gloucester's fantastic supporters gave him a rousing cheer. The team deserved their day in the sun, and there is no danger of Walkinshaw selling off the family silver.

Gloucester: T Delport; M Garvey, T Fanolua, H Paul (P Todd, 74), J Simpson-Daniel, L Mercier, A Gomarsall; T Woodman, O Azam, A Deacon, A Eustace, R Fidler, J Boer (capt), J Forrester, A Hazell (J Paramore, 60; E Pearce, 74).

Northampton: N Beal; B McRama, P Jorgensen (C Hyndman, 67), J Leslie (co-capt), B Cohen; P Grayson, M Dawson; T Smith, S Thompson, R Morris (M Stewart, 55), M Lord, S Williams, M Connors (D Fox, 76), A Blowers, B Pountney (co-capt).

Referee: T Spreadbury (Somerset).

M

MELVILLE

Former Director of Coaching, Nigel Melville's record while at Gloucester Rugby Club was as follows:

Home

Season	Played	Won	Drew	Lost	Points For	Against
2001-02	2	2	0	0	128	21
2002-03	16	16	0	0	560	233
2003-04	17	15	0	2	492	269
2004-05	17	10	0	7	369	329
TOTAL	52	43	0	9	1549	852

Away

Season	Played	Won	Drew	Lost	Points For	Against
2001-02	6	4	0	2	200	177
2002-03	17	9	2	6	443	404
2003-04	14	5	0	9	272	340
2004-05	16	6	1	9	281	363
TOTAL	53	24	3	26	1196	1284

Overall

Played	Won	Drew	Lost	Point For	Against
105	67	3	35	2745	2136

MORE AND MORE MEDALS

During a five season stay at Kingsholm, Henry Paul collected more medals than any other player in that time that were members of the Club's playing staff. Henry's honours came thus:

2001-2002	Championship Final	–	Winner
2002-2003	Premiership Final	–	Loser
2002-2003	Powergen Cup	–	Winner
2002	Hong Kong Sevens	–	Winner
2003	Hong Kong Sevens	–	Winner

He was also capped six times by England: 2002 v France (Replacement), 2004 v Italy (Replacement), v Scotland (Replacement), 2004 v Canada, 2004 v Australia, and v South Africa.

MAURICE McCANLIS

Maurice McCanlis, the Club's former centre three quarter who made 95 appearances for the Club scoring 28 tries between 1928-1936 appeared for Gloucestershire C.C.C. and Surrey C.C.C. scoring 2,612 runs at an average of 32-21. He also took 82 wickets. It must be pointed out that he made one solitary appearance for this County.

ON THE MARK

Mark Mapletoft, the former Gloucester R.F.C. utility back was a prolific point scorer for the Club:

1994-1995 – 85 points, 1995-96 – 203 points, 1996-97 – 209 points, 1997-98 – 275 points, 1998-99 – 198 points.

It was during the 1998-99 season he scored his 100th point for the Club achieving this target on 2nd March 1998.

His achievement set a record for it was accumulated in 86 appearances. John Liley, then of Leicester R.F.C. held the previous record for he had reached his milestone in 92 matches.

Ironically it was versus Leicester in a Cheltenham and Gloucester Cup Match that Mark recorded his personal triumph. In five seasons at Kingsholm he registered 848 points.

LUDO ON THE MARK

Former Gloucester Rugby Club fly half Ludovic Mercier amassed more than 500 points in his first spell with the Club and became the second fastest player to reach 500 premiership points. He achieved this in 36 matches, one more than Barry Everitt then of London Irish. Ludo scored 34 points in the Zurich Championship Quarter Final against Newcastle in 2002. Ludo is in sixth position of all time records in League Rugby Union with 64 penalties in a season. Barry Everitt of London Irish holds the record with 83 in the 2001-2002 season, Ludo recorded his penalties in the same season. When Ludovic Mercier scored 42 conversions in the 2002-2003 season he became only the second player to score more than 40 conversions in a season. Ludovic recorded 48 in 2001/2002 and joined Jon Callard then of Bath R.F.C. as the only player to achieve this feat.

MILITARY MEDALS

Military medals won by Gloucester Rugby players were Henry Berry – Queens Medal, Peter Hordern – Air Force Cross, Percy Stout – Distinguished Service Order, Christopher Champion Tanner – Albert Medal, Frank Stout – Military Cross.

EVENTUALLY A CAP FOR MELVILLE

Former Gloucester Rugby Director of Coaching, Nigel Melville, toured with the British Lions in 1983 to New Zealand before being capped by England on 3rd November 1984.

THE GREAT MARCH

Virtually all the players of the Club joined the 5th Gloucestershire Regiment in 1914 to fight in the Great War and march into France.

MORE THE MERRIER

Matches played reached a premium in the 1969/70 season when 57 first XV games were played.

MERIT TABLE

The 'Merit Table' run by the Sunday Telegraph and the Daily Mail saw Gloucester Rugby Football Club placed top of this unofficial League in 1983.

MAJOR INVESTOR

A major investor was sought by the Club in the 1995/96 season as they found themselves adrift from other professional clubs and therefore lost ground to opponents in recruiting players and also from acquiring revenue.

MAY TIME

In May 1996 the Club transformed itself into a Limited Company. The Board of Directors included two full time Executive Directors, a Managing Director and a Rugby Director.

ON THE MARK

Mark Mapletoft is Gloucester's top point's scorer in league rugby. More than 500 of his 836 points were recorded at Kingsholm.

FIVE FOR ENGLAND MATCHES

Five players with their surnames beginning with the letter 'M' have played for England – Maurice McCanlis, Neil McCarthy, Mark Mapletoft, Steve Mills and Olly Morgan.

ALL THE M's

Opponents have been: Maesteg, Manchester, Maritime, Middlesex Wanderers, Milano, Morecombe, Moseley and Munster.

MILLS WITHOUT THE FRILLS

Steve Mills, the Gloucester Rugby Football Club hooker in 1987 was capped by England when they were the first of the Home Countries to take advantage of a new International Board ruling to the effect that members may award full caps for games against non I.B. countries. Caps were awarded on 30th May 1981 in Buenos Aeries versus Argentina to Steve and his Gloucester Rugby Club colleague John Fidler.

MELVILLE APPOINTMENT

Former Wasps Director of Coaching, Nigel Melville, was appointed in a similar role at Kingsholm in March 2002.

MAKING A DUO

McGregor and Mynott were the first All Black players to appear for Gloucester Rugby Football Club versus Leicester in 1905 on 13th January.

NATIONAL CUP WINNERS – M

Ludovic Mercier	2003
Steve Mills	1978, 1982
Richard Mogg	1978, 1982
Roy Morris	1972

A WINNER

Prior to joining Gloucester Rugby Club, Nigel Melville had managed the England Under-21s, won a League Championship and two domestic Cup Finals at Twickenham with Wasps.

MANAGING DIRECTOR

Managing Director, Ken Nottage, moved to Kingsholm in June 1999. Previous to joining Gloucester Rugby Club he was with Newcastle whom he had joined in April 1996. Ken succeeded Hamish Brown.

NEIL McCARTHY

Former Gloucester and England hooker, Neil McCarthy made League appearances for all three West Country clubs, Bath, Bristol and Gloucester. The Leeds Grammar School educated player was the 1,210[th] player to represent England at International level.

ALL THE MEADOWS

There have been seven players with the surname of Meadows who have appeared in the first team for Gloucester R.F.C. They are: D. Meadow 1953, Don Meadows (1927-1938), F. Meadows (1921-1923), Howard Meadows (1946-50), J. Meadows (1910-1913), L. C. Meadows (1927-1929) and P. Meadows (1964-1968).

AND THE MORGAN'S

There have been nine players with the surname of Morgan who have made appearances in the Club's 1st XV: A. Morgan (1893-1896), D. Morgan (1954-55), H. Morgan (1932-1933), L. F. Morgan (1899-1903), L. S. G. Morgan (1952-1955), M. Morgan (1955), I. Morgan (1987-1991), O. Morgan (2005-), and D. Morgan

MILITARY MEN ON PATROL AT KINGSHOLM

Those who have served in the Armed Forces and had their military rank included in the Club annals are the following: Sgt. Maj. E. Beavon played for the 1st XV in 1946 and 1947. During that time he made 30 appearances scoring three tries. Captain F. E. Clarke made two appearances for the Club in 1919. A Flight Lieutenant Gibbs made a solitary appearance in 1945; Captain D. Gilbert-Smith appeared for the Club in 1961 and 1962 making 17 appearances and recording four tries.

A Lieutenant Hone made just one appearance for Gloucester R.F.C. in 1928. In that same season with the equivalent rank Lieutenant Nott also made that same solitary appearance.

Prior to their sole appearance, Major W. Roderick had outflanked them by making 49 appearances between 1921 and 1923 recording three tries in the process.

MIDDLESEX SEVENS

Gloucester Rugby Club won the Compass Group Middlesex Sevens Tournament on Saturday 13th August 2005 when they defeated London Wasps in the Final at Twickenham by 35 points to 26. The full squad who participated were:

Simon Amor (Captain), James Bailey, Will Matthews, Olly Morgan, James Forrester, Jake Boer, Marcel Garvey, Brad Davies, Luke Narraway and Anthony Allen.

CAPTAIN 'M'

Players who have been appointed Club Captain with their surname commencing with the letter 'M' are:

Tom Millington (1923-24), Don Meadows (1936-37), Roy Morris in conjunction with Tom Price in (1946-47).

MORE!

The only clubs to have had more players capped by England are Blackheath, Harlequins, Oxford University, Cambridge University, Leicester and Richmond. These are the only six clubs Gloucester Rugby Club trail!

MERRY CHRISTMAS

When Leicester visited Kingsholm in December 1992 it was the 2,167[th] match to be played at Kingsholm and was the 4,047[th] in the Club's history.

N

NICHOLLS – ALMOST EVER PRESENT

Former Gloucester hooker and Club Captain Mike Nicholls played in 52 of the Club's 54 first team fixtures in the 1973-74 season.

NOTHING NEW

The New Zealand touring team of 1905-06 defeated Gloucester R.F.C. at Kingsholm by 44 points with no reply.

NATIONAL CUP

The R.F.U. National Cup has been won on four occasions in the years of 1972, 1978, 1982 and 2003.

OH NEWPORT

In the season of 1888/89 the Club had to cancel fixtures with Welsh club Newport. This was following violence from both their players and spectators.

NUMBERS

Numbers were used on Gloucester shirts for the first time when New Zealand were the visitors to Kingsholm on 10th October 1905.

NO NON-LOCALS

Non local players caused concern in the 1913-14 season but the Club admitted 'that gates would dwindle considerably'.

NETHERLANDS

The Club appeared in a tournament at Leiden, Netherlands at the commencement of the 1992-93 season defeating Cascais (Portugal) 50-21 and losing to Bridgend (Wales) by 22 points to twelve.

ALL THE N's

Opponents have been: Neath, New Zealand, Newbridge, New Brighton, Newcastle, Northampton, Northern, North Gloucester Combination, Northern Transvaal and Nottingham.

NATIONAL CUP WINNERS – N

Mike Nicholls   1972

NIL

The only match in which Gloucester Rugby Club failed to register a single point while Nigel Melville was Director of Coaching was in a Heineken European Cup match at Kingsholm on 16th January 2005 versus Stade Francais in a 27-0 defeat.

DEBUTANT NIGEL

Former Gloucester Rugby Director of Coaching Nigel Melville was Captain of England on his debut versus Australia at Twickenham on 3 November 1984. The Australians were victors by 19 points to three. Nigel became the first England player to captain the national team on his debut since Joe Mycock in 1947. Steve Mills of Gloucester was also included in that England team as hooker.

NO TITLE

When Gloucester Rugby Club completed the 2002-2003 season they were clear and runaway winners of the Premiership by 15 clear points. Their playing record was:

Played	22
Won	17
Drew	2
Lost	3
Points For	617
Points Against	396
Tries For	67
Tries Against	35
Try Bonus	7
Losing Bonus	3
League Points	82

Unfortunately the previous season it had been decided that there would be a playoff system introduced. Only one of the 12 clubs voted against the system – Leicester. London Wasps won the play off final defeating Gloucester 39-3 on 31st May 2003 at Twickenham. Four years later it occurred again with Leicester handing out another severe defeat at Twickenham by 44-16 on 12th May 2007.

NINTH

Prior to today's seven named replacements Clubs were restricted to one replacement named as – ninth forward!

CAPTAIN 'N'

Players who have been appointed Club Captain with their surname commencing with the letter 'N' have been:

Mike Nicholls   1970-71, 1971-72, 1973-74

NOT AT HOME

In the 1971-72 season in the R.F.U. Knock Out Cup the Club were never drawn at home. Each round was played away from Kingsholm. Not to be deterred they triumphed to lift the Cup at Twickenham by a winning margin of 17-6. The results were Bath won 12-3, Bristol 15-4, Coventry drew 6-6 progressing on the away rule, London Welsh won 9-4. In the final at Twickenham Moseley was defeated 17 points to six. The team facing Moseley was:

E. J. Stephens, R. J. Clewes, J. A. Bayliss, R. Morris, J. Dix, T. Palmer, M. H. Booth, R. J. Cowling, M. J. Nicholls (Captain), M. A. Burton, J. S. Jarrett, A. Brinn, J. A. Watkins, M. J. Potter, R. Smith.

Try scorers: J. Dix, R. Morris
Drop goals: T. Palmer, M. H. Booth
Penalty: E. J. Stephens

NOMADIC

Former Gloucester Rugby Club scrum half Peter Richards has appeared for Bristol, Wasps, London Irish (twice) and Harlequins. He has appeared for England at every level. He was voted Player of the Dubai Sevens tournament 2004.

NATIONAL CUP WINNERS AGAIN

The Cherry and Whites lifted the Cup again for the second time in the 1977-78 competition. It was a less arduous route than in 1971-72. Only R. J. Clewes, M. A. Burton and J. A. Watkins remained of that earlier triumph as they faced Leicester in the final. To reach Twickenham they had defeated High Wycombe at Kingsholm 40 points to six in the Third Round. Exeter at Kingsholm 34 points to three in Round 4. In the quarter final they defeated Sale 13-6 at home and defeated Coventry 18 points to nine away in the Semi-Final.

Team: P. E. Butler, R. J. Clewes, B. J. Vine, R. Jardine, R. R. Mogg, C. J. Williams, P. R. Howell, G. A. F. Sargent, S. G. F. Mills, M. A. Burton, S. B. Boyle, J. H. Fidler, J. A. Watkins (Captain), J. F. Simonett and V. J. Wooley.

NEUTRAL VENUES

Gloucester Rugby Club have played at neutral venues over the years, obviously more so in the professional era. The list includes:

European Shield Semi-Final
Franklin Gardens, Northampton
Gloucester 27 – Sale 28

28th April 2002

Cheltenham & Gloucester Cup Final
Franklin Gardens, Northampton
Bedford 25 – Gloucester 33

3rd April 1998

Guinness Premiership League
Ashton Gate, Bristol
Gloucester 35 – Bristol 13

28th April 2007

Cheltenham & Gloucester Cup Final
Franklin Gardens, Northampton
Bedford 9 – Gloucester 24

9th April 1999

Zurich Championship Final
Twickenham
Bristol 23 – Gloucester 28

8th June 2002

Zurich Wild Card Semi-Final
Twickenham
Gloucester 16 – Saracens 24

14th May 2005

Heineken Cup Semi-Final
Vicarage Road, Watford
Gloucester 15 – Leicester 19

21st April 2001

Powergen Cup Semi-Final
Franklin Gardens, Northampton
Gloucester 16 – Leicester 11

1st March 2003

Powergen Cup Final
Twickenham
Gloucester 40 – Northampton 22

5th April 2003

Zurich Championship Final
Twickenham
Gloucester 3 – Wasps 39

31st May 2003

European Challenge Final
The Stoop
Gloucester 36 – London Irish 34 (After Extra Time)

21st May 2006

Guinness Premiership Final	12th May 2006

Twickenham
Gloucester 16 – Leicester 44

E.D.F. Energy Cup Semi-Final	28th March 2009

Ricoh Stadium, Coventry
Gloucester 17 – Ospreys 0

E.D.F. Energy Cup Final	18th April 2009

Twickenham
Cardiff 50 – Gloucester 12

NOTHING TO DECLARE

There have been 59 matches during the Club's history where we have been involved in matches where they have ended pointless. Those thirty matches are as follows since we commenced playing at Kingsholm:

1891-92	Oxford University (Away), Penarth (Home)
1894-95	Leicester (Home), Bristol (Away)
1895-96	Swansea (Home), Old Merchant Taylors (Home), Bath (Home)
1896-97	Penarth (Away), Coventry (Away), Cinderford (Home)
1897-98	Llanelli (Home), Newport (Home), Devonport Albion (Away)
1898-99	Cinderford (Away)
1899-00	Coventry (Away), Leicester (Home)
1900-01	Penarth (Away), Newport (Home), Old Merchant Taylors (Home)
1901-02	Newport (Home)
1903-04	Devonport Albion (Away)
1904-05	Devonport Albion (Home)
1905-06	Cinderford (Away)
1908-09	Swansea (Home)
1909-10	Cinderford (Away), Leicester (Away), Neath (Home)
1910-11	Bristol (Away)
1912-13	Cinderford (Away)
1913-14	Cheltenham (Away)
1919-20	Lydney (Away)
1921-22	Swansea (Home)
1922-23	Pontypool (Home)
1924-25	Lydney (Home)
1927-28	Lydney (Away)

1930-31	Lydney (Home), Llanelli (Home), Cheltenham (Away)
1931-32	Cheltenham (Away)
1932-33	Lydney (Away)
1933-34	Devonport Services (Away)
1936-37	Cheltenham (Away), Bristol (Home)
1938-39	Llanelli (Home)
1948-49	Northampton (Away)
1949-50	Llanelli (Home)
1950-51	Cheltenham (Home), Bristol (Home), United Services (Away), Lydney (Away)
1951-52	Stroud (Home)
1955-56	Swansea (Home)
1956-57	Cheltenham (Home), Swansea (Away)
1960-61	Old Blues (Home), Lydney (Away)
1966-67	Coventry (Home)
1970-71	Bath (Away)
1976-77	London Scottish (Home)

31 of those matches were played at Kingsholm, 28 away.

Fanolua facing a family reunion

by Katie Coker

WESTERN Samoan Junior Paramore will clash with his cousin Terry Fanolua when Bedford meet Gloucester in the Cheltenham and Gloucester Cup final on Friday.

Paramore, who usually plays in the back row, has been selected in the centre because Bedford have several players unavailable through injury or international call-ups.

The two Western Samoan internationals' mothers are sisters and they spent a lot of time together even though 29-year-old Paramore is six years older than Fanolua.

Paramore joined Bedford in 1996 and Fanolua followed him to England last summer. The two have played in the same Western Samoan team, but never against one another.

Fanolua was out of the country when

Gloucester lost 32-20 to Bedford in a friendly match at Kingsholm at the end of February, so he is looking forward to facing Paramore and helping Gloucester exact their revenge.

"Junior and I are good friends," said Fanolua.

"He hasn't given me any stick about Bedford beating Gloucester a few weeks ago. I was overseas then, so I wasn't playing.

"I have been to a few of Bedford's games this year and he is a big part of their team. He is a good ball player, and he is a powerful runner and a good tackler as well," said Fanolua.

"Bedford really use him a lot. He is a top player. His work-rate is pretty high

and he is a vital member of the Bedford team. We are looking to beat them on Friday for revenge and to win a bit of silverware as well."

Paramore said: "I see Terry a lot now he plays in England, and have seen Gloucester a few times, so I know what to expect.

"I have offered to put Terry up in Bedford for the weekend, but if they win then I might withdraw that offer.

"Being up against him will add a little bit of spice in the match, and although we will be best friends afterwards, he knows what to expect during it."

BEDFORD (v Gloucester, at Northampton, Friday, 8pm): M. Rayer, B. Whetstone, J. Paramore, M. Pechey, R. Underwood; P. Turner, S. Crabb; N. Hatley, J. Richards, C. Boyd, S. Murray, S. Platford, R. Winters, J. Forster, R. Straeuli. Reps from: S. Brading, R. Stone, S. Howard, A. Davis, J. Cullen, D. Hinkins, M. Deans.

O

OLD BILL

For the England v Wales match played at Kingsholm in 1900, the first International played at Kingsholm, the Club had no fewer than 50 coppers at one shilling per hair per head. The bill came to £15.00. One hundred years later six constables cost £1,000.00 per match.

OH DEAR

Did you know that in the Spring of 1894 an All Star team played at Kingsholm? It was billed as Wales and Gloucester versus Yorkshire. The Northern team included Walter Jackson, a nimble footed and speedy three quarter who had been a regular Gloucester player until he joined Halifax after the 1892/93 season. Following the match the Gloucester Captain J. Harman took part in a Boxing match at the Gloucester Corn Exchange against a Morgan Crowther.

OPENING DAY

The Cherry and Whites had a run of 42 seasons where they won the opening game of each season. That run started in 1894-95 with a win against Morecambe at Kingsholm and ended with a drawn match in 1949-50 at home to Lydney. The overall record for matches played as the opening game of each season reads: WON 89, DREW 2 LOST 16. The two draws were versus Lydney 3-3 in 1949-50 and Worcester in 2005-06 in a fifteen points apiece encounter. Only 16 defeats in a 107 match run is no mean feat.

Home matches are in capital letters.

1891-92	Stratford-on-Avon	Won	22-10
1892-93	BRISTOL	Won	14-0
1893-94	BRISTOL	Lost	3-7
1894-95	MORECAMBE	Won	14-3
1895-96	CARDIFF & DISTRICT	Lost	0-3
1896-97	CHELTENHAM	Won	12-0
1897-98	CLIFTON	Won	14-0
1898-99	CLIFTON	Won	18-0
1899-1900	CLIFTON	Won	30-8

1900-01	CLIFTON	Won	66-0
1901-02	CLIFTON	Won	74-0
1902-03	CLIFTON	Won	45-0
1903-04	STROUD	Won	5-0
1904-05	OLD EDWARDIANS	Won	45-0
1905-06	CLIFTON	Won	29-0
1906-07	LYDNEY	Won	6-0
1907-08	CLIFTON	Won	38-10
1908-09	Plymouth	Won	219

1909-10	PENARTH	Won	11-6
1910-11	BREAM	Won	30-5
1911-12	PENYCRAIG	Won	27-0
1912-13	BREAM	Won	29-0
1913-14	BREAM	Won	7-3
1919-20	LYDNEY	Won	13-3
1920-21	LYDNEY	Won	17-0
1921-22	LYDNEY	Won	23-0
1922-23	LYDNEY	Won	11-0

1923-24	LYDNEY	Won	43-12
1924-25	Lydney	Drew	0-0
1925-26	Stroud	Won	19-3
1926-27	Stroud	Won	8-3
1927-28	Stroud	Won	8-0

1928-29	Stroud	Won	18-0
1929-30	Stroud	Won	18-6
1930-31	Stroud	Won	26-3
1931-32	Stroud	Won	9-3

1932-33	Stroud	Won	9-0
1933-34	Moseley	Won	16-5
1934-35	LYDNEY	Won	22-6
1935-36	LYDNEY	Won	21-3
1936-37	LYDNEY	Won	16-3
1937-38	LYDNEY	Won	30-3
1938-39	LYDNEY	Won	17-3
1939-40	GLOUCESTERSHIRE REGIMENT	Won	29-9
1945-46	BRISTOL	Won	18-0

1946-47	LYDNEY	Won	30-3
1947-48	LYDNEY	Won	23-8
1948-49	LYDNEY	Won	29-12
1949-50	LYDNEY	Drew	3-3
1950-51	LYDNEY	Lost	3-8
1951-52	LYDNEY	Won	11-3
1952-53	Stourbridge	Won	19-14
1953-54	Stourbridge	Won	22-3
1954-55	LYDNEY	Won	11-0

1955-56	LYDNEY	Won	16-6
1956-57	LYDNEY	Won	15-8
1957-58	WATERLOO	Won	11-3
1958-59	LYDNEY	Won	40-8
1959-60	STROUD	Lost	14-17
1960-61	WATERLOO	Won	26-14
1961-62	LYDNEY	Won	26-3
1962-63	Torquay	Won	21-9
1963-64	Neath	Lost	0-6

1964-65	WATERLOO	Won	9-3
1965-66	BROUGHTON PARK	Lost	12-14
1966-67	CLIFTON	Won	15-6
1967-68	LYDNEY	Won	18-6
1968-69	LYDNEY	Won	54-6
1969-70	PHILADELPHIA UNIVERSITY	Won	60-0
1970-71	CLIFTON	Won	26-3
1971-72	CLIFTON	Won	26-11
1972-73	Broughton Park	Won	14-4

1973-74	Broughton Park	Lost	24-33
1974-75	BROUGHTON PARK	Won	31-3
1975-76	Weston-Super-Mare	Won	37-3
1976-77	BROUGHTON PARK	Won	31-6
1977-78	Broughton Park	Won	27-0
1978-79	BROUGHTON PARK	Won	33-4
1979-80	Broughton Park	Won	16-9
1980-81	BROUGHTON PARK	Won	26-19
1981-82	New Brighton	Won	58-4

1982-83	Stroud	Lost	16-21
1983-84	STROUD	Won	26-6
1984-85	SWANSEA	Lost	19-20
1985-86	Exeter	Won	36-13
1986-87	Cinderford	Won	24-6
1987-88	Swansea	Won	19-6
1988-89	SWANSEA	Won	35-13
1989-90	SWANSEA	Won	32-29
1990-91	SWANSEA	Lost	4-14

1991-92	STROUD	Won	54-3
1992-93	Coscais (Portugal)	Won	50-21
1993-94	Lydney	Lost	0-3
1994-95	Hamiltons	Lost	23-27
1995-96	WAKEFIELD	Won	39-12

1996-97	PONTYPRIDD	Won	15-5
1997-98	Begles-Bordeaux	Lost	31-32
1998-99	LONDON IRISH	Won	29-22
1999-2000	NEWCASTLE	Won	31-16

2000-01	Saracens	Lost	20-50
2001-02	NORTHAMPTON	Won	22-9
2002-03	Harlequins	Won	25-19
2003-04	ROTHERHAM	Won	22-8
2004-05	Leeds	Won	21-16
2005-06	Worcester	Drew	15-15
2006-07	BATH	Won	24-19
2007-08	Leeds	Won	49-24
2008-09	LEICESTER	Lost	8-20

O.M.T.'s

Rugby Union on a Christmas holiday belongs to a bygone era. The most frequent visitors to Kingsholm were Old Merchant Taylors. In all they played 62 matches against this Club before the fixture was terminated in 1973. The visit of that year resulted in a Gloucester win by a then Kingsholm record 82 points to twelve margin. Although there was one other visit when Old Merchant Taylors celebrated their Centenary in the 1982-93 season requesting a visit to Kingsholm. That was the 63rd and final meeting. Gloucester R.F.C. inflicting a 70 points to nil defeat. In actual fact the O.M.T.'s paid their first visit to Gloucester in 1890 when the fixture was played at the Spa. Gloucester winning by a try and three minors to a minor. This was the only fixture not to be played at Kingsholm.

OLD PROGRAMMES

It is generally believed that the oldest programme of this Club was printed in 1900. The oldest in existence is believed to be of 1904. The programme of 1900 cost 1d. The Gloucester team was printed in comic form as follows:

BACK

Red and Jack	W. Hodges

THREE QUARTER BACK

Giles Farmer	G. Romans
A. Lazybones	R. Cole
Charley Wallpaper	P. G. Harris
A. Notout	F. Rust

HALFBACKS

Our Slavey	R. G. Haris
Little Titch	P. Rodway

FORWARDS

Segt Coppem	A. Purton
Becky Pilgrim	H. Richardson
Farmer Two Cows	C. Walwin
Alice Whereartthou	J. Welshman
Andy Andy	W. Smith
Convict 99	G. Vance
V. Davie	T. B. Phillips

ONLY TWO O's

Two players with their surname commencing with 'O' have represented England – Steve Ojomoh and John Orwin.

ALL THE O's

Opponents have been: Old Blues, Old Cranleighans, Old Crocks, Old Edwardians, Old Merchant Taylors, Old Paulines, Old Regatians, Orrell, Oxford Greyhounds, Oxford University and Ospreys.

JOHN ORWIN

Former Gloucester lock forward John Orwin was a member of the England team that on 19th March 1988 defeated Ireland by 35 points to three at Twickenham in the final match of the Five Nations Championship. It was their then biggest winning margin over the Irish. The England team were captained by Nigel Melville, later to be appointed as Director of Coaching at Gloucester Rugby Club. This was the match that 'Swing Low, Sweet Chariot' was first heard from a Twickenham crowd.

722

GLOUCESTER RUGBY FOOTBALL CLUB

Founded 1873

PRESIDENT: A. T. VOYCE, OBE

GLOUCESTER

v

CAMBRIDGE UNIVERSITY

KINGSHOLM, GLOUCESTER

SATURDAY, 25th JANUARY, 1975

Kick-Off: 3.00 p.m.

Price: 5p

Match programme for the 1975 game between Gloucester and Cambridge University

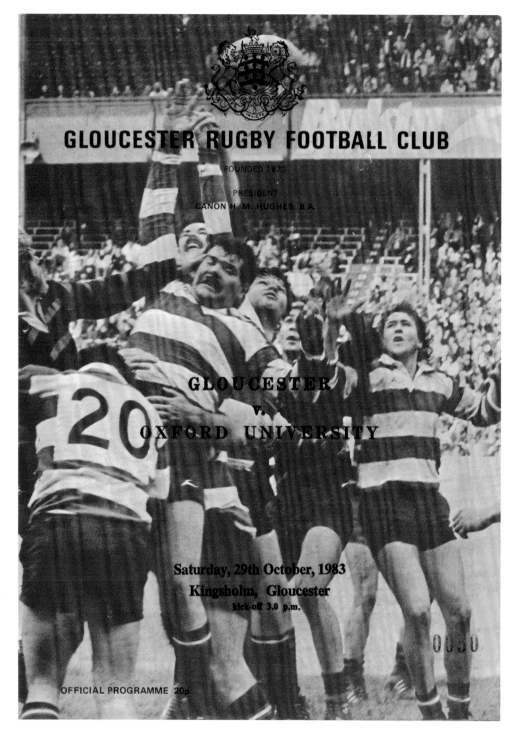

GLOUCESTER RUGBY FOOTBALL CLUB

FOUNDED 1873

PRESIDENT
CANON H. M. HUGHES, B.A.

GLOUCESTER
v.
OXFORD UNIVERSITY

Saturday, 29th October, 1983
Kingsholm, Gloucester
kick-off 3.0 p.m.

0050

OFFICIAL PROGRAMME 20p

Match programme for the 1983 fixture between Gloucester and Oxford
University at Kingsholm

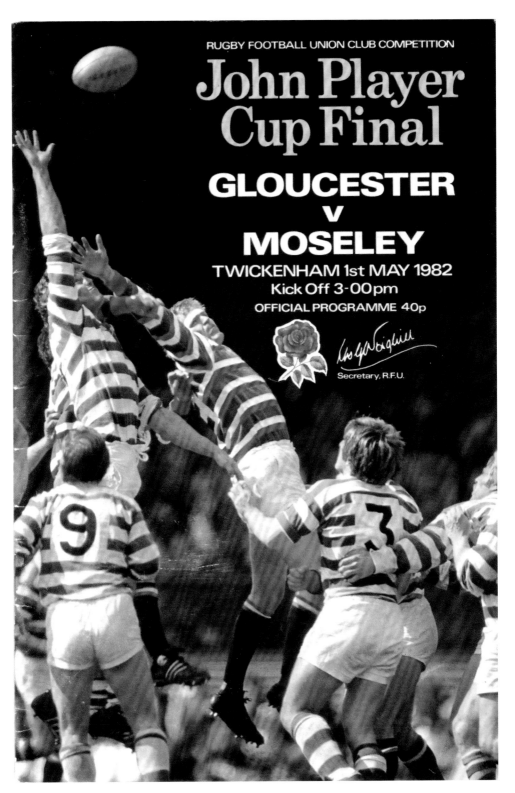

Programme for the 1982 Gloucester versus Mosely fixture

Alex Brown

Andy Gormasall

Andy Hazell

James Simpson-Daniel

Dave Sims

Above: Gloucester Cathedral
seen through the posts at
Kingsholm

Right: Neil McCarthy

Gloucester win the line out versus West Hartlepool in 1995. Tony Windo, the Gloucester prop, is in the foreground on the left. The old changing quarters

can be seen in the background. Dave Sims, Gloucester's first professional
player, is in the foreground on the right.

Henry Paul

Ian Smith

The main grandstand being removed in 2007

The Buildbase Stand in 2008

CLOUCESTER RUGBY FOOTBALL TEAM. 1904-5.

W. H. Taylor, J. Harrison, F. Goulding, G. Matthews, G. Vears, B. Hawker, W. Johns, F. Pegler, T. Bagwell (Tr iner)
G. H. Smith, A. Hudson, G. Romans (Capt.) C. Smith, B. Parham, T. Leonard,
E, Hall, D. Gent, J. Stephens.

Then and now: Above is the team photograph for the 1904-1905 season;
the photograph below shows the 2001-2002 squad

L-R: Scott Benton, Tom Walkinshaw, Phil Greening, Mark Mapletoft and
Richard Hill

Pre-season preparation of the pitch

England and former Gloucester squad member, Phil Vickery

Gloucester R.F.C. on a tour of the city following their Powergen Cup win in 2003

CAPTAIN JOHN ORWIN

John Orwin, then of Bedford, captained England for the first time on 23rd April 1988 against Ireland at Lansdowne Road, Dublin in a match which was staged as part of the Dublin Millennium celebrations. England were victors by 21 points to ten. Along with Mike Harrison of Wakefield they are the only players to have captained England from outside the top division in League rugby.

NATIONAL CUP WINNERS – O

John Orwin   1982

OVERSEAS LEADER!

The first overseas player to captain the Club was Australian centre Richard Tombs.

OJOMOH SAW THE LIGHT

Steve Ojomoh, former Gloucester back row forward, played in England's first match under floodlight during the 1995 World Cup in Durban, South Africa, against Argentina on 27th May 1995. A match England won by 24 points to eighteen, with Rob Andrew scoring all of England's points.

OLD SPOT!

Was an independent Match Day Newsletter based at Newbrook House, Queen's Road, Stonehouse, Gloucestershire in 1996-97 and cost 50 pence. It was published by Newsbrook Publications, Newbrook House, Stonehouse. It was sold outside of Kingsholm on match days and appeared to be an alternative to the Club programme containing the match day teams, appearances and scorers of that season and also career details. It also included League tables and a full fixture list along with articles and letters to the Editor.

ADRIAN OLVER

The former Gloucester Rugby Club prop forward has appeared for five different clubs in the Premiership – Saracens, Bedford, Rotherham, Harlequins and Gloucester.

CAPTAIN 'O'

Players who have been appointed Club Captain with their surname commencing with the letter 'O' have been:

John Orwin   1984-85, 1985-86.

OUTSTANDING

Steve Ojomoh, the former Gloucester back row forward was an outstanding athlete at school. He was the South West Schools Champion at Discus, Long Jump and Triple Jump. He became all England Schools Decathlon Bronze Medallist in 1988. Steve was born in Benin City, Nigeria in 1964 and educated at West Buckland School, Devon.

ONE/TWO

'Dick' Smith played in the first R.F.U. National Cup Final of 1972 and his son Ian played in the 1990 Cup Final versus Bath.

ORRELL

The only club to have failed to register a single point against Gloucester R.F.C. in the professional era at Kingsholm are Orrell who lost 27-0 in the 1995-96 season and by 30-0 in the following season of 1996-97.

OFFICIALS

In 1992-93 the Club officials were all former players of this Club.
Chairman: Peter Ford, Hon. Secretary, Doug Wadley, Hon Fixture Secretary, Mike Nicholls.
Chairman of Selectors: Mickey Booth
Coach: Keith Richardson

P

PLAYER OF THE SEASON

The awards were introduced at the end of the 2001/2002 season under the auspices of the Season Ticket Holders Association. The following have been given their awards prior to an end of season match:

2001-2002   Ludovic Mercier
2002-2003   Jake Boer

For the next season it was decided to introduce a Young Player of the Season award.

	PLAYER OF SEASON	YOUNG PLAYER OF SEASON
2003/2004	Henry Paul	Jon Goodridge
2004/2005	Adam Balding	Nick Wood
2005/2006	Andy Hazell	Olly Morgan
2006/2007	Andy Hazell	Anthony Allen
2007/2008	James Simpson-Daniel	Ryan Lamb
2008/2009	Olivier Azam	Olly Morgan

HENRY PAUL

Prior to joining Gloucester R.F.C. Henry Paul had enjoyed a successful Rugby League career. Henry joined Wakefield Trinity in 1993 from Te Atatu in New Zealand. He played 19 games, scoring 7 tries, 41 goals and 1 drop goal for a points total of 111.

He then joined Wigan, where he stayed until the end of 1998. Henry made 141 appearances and 6 substitute appearances for Wigan scoring 78 tries, 119 goals for a total of 550 points.

Henry joined Bradford Bulls in 1999. In his three years at the Club he made 95 + 5 substitute appearances scoring 32 tries, 416 goals and 7 drop goals for a total of 967 points. Of all the players who have joined Gloucester Rugby Club from Rugby League, Henry is the most successful. His career statistics at Kingsholm read:

Season	Appearances	Tries	Conversions	Dropped Goals	Penalties	Points
2001-02	20 + 2	5	34	0	9	120
2002-03	29+2	6	6	0	11	75
2003-04	29	4	52	1	73	346
2004-05	24	3	28	2	55	242
2005-06	5	0	0	0	0	0
TOTALS	107+4	18	120	3	148	783

BEFORE PAY

Until the advent of the professional game of Rugby Union there had been in place a League system of National recognition. The Club's leading points scorers and try scorers up until 1996 were:

Season	Points	Point Scorer	Try Scorer	Tries
1987-88	42	Nick Marment	Jim Breeze	6
1988-89	85	Tim Smith	Mike Hamlin	6
1989-90	75	Tim Smith	Derek Morgan	6
1990-91	75	Tim Smith	Ian Smith	3
			Derek Morgan	3
			Paul Ashmead	3
			Chris Dee	3
1991-92	81	Tim Smith	Simon Morris	5
1992-93	71	Tim Smith	Tim Smith	3
1993-94	82	Tim Smith	Paul Holford	3
			Bruce Fenley	3
1994-95	85	Mark Mapletoft	Paul Holford	8
1995-96	79	Tim Smith	Mike Lloyd	7

PLAYER OF THE YEAR

The Player of the Season award in the Rothmans awards for 1997-98 went to former Gloucester prop forwards Christian Califano who was then playing for Stade Toulousain. At the time the 26 year old French International loosehead was regarded as the best prop forward in the world of Rugby Union. Christian was born in Toulon where he played for six years before joining Stade Toulousain. The now 37 year old who later played for Saracens returned to Toulouse to live when he retired from the game at the completion of the 2007-08 season. Christian was capped 71 times by France in an International career which stretched from 1994 when he made his debut versus New Zealand until 2007 when he played his final Test Match ironically also against the famous 'All Blacks'. A career length only equalled in French International Rugby by F. Haget. Only six players have been awarded more caps than Christian by France.

PHILIPPE A TRY SCORER

Former Gloucester wing three-quarter Philippe St Andre scored 32 tries from his 69 International appearances for France. A total which only twelve players have surpassed.

AT A PRICE

There have been seven players with the surname of Price who have played for Gloucester R.F.C. in the 1st XV. They are:

C. Price (1947), F. Price (1928-1930), J. Price (1909), J. R. Price (1891-1895), M. Price (1964), T. Price (1934-1937) and N. Price (1982-1993).

PATROLLING!

J. R. Price who played for the Kingsholm Club between 1891 and 1895, made 80 appearances and scoring eight tries. He made his debut for the Club on 3rd October 1891 versus Stratford. His last appearance came at Coventry on 23rd November 1896. The former Gloucestershire County forward was told to rejoin the Grenadier Guards in 1900 on official orders, he duly obeyed!

POLICEMEN ON DUTY

When Gloucester faced Gosforth in a second round clash of the 1977-78 National Knock Out Cup, John Fidler was out jumping fellow policeman John Hedley in the lineout despite the Gosforth lock being four inches taller. A 19-10 victory ensued.

CAPTAIN 'P'

Players with their surname commencing with the letter 'P' who have been appointed Club Captains are:

Malcolm Preedy 1986-87

PATERSON

Chris Paterson, the Club's utility back stretched his perfect place kicking run in test matches to 33 out of 33 in last seasons Six Nations. That tally equalled the world record of Canada's Jared Barker who slotted his kicks between June and August 2002.

PARKER

Former Gloucester R.F.C. and England's full back Graham Parker who played for the Club (1931-36) and made 64 appearances scoring eleven tries, converting 35 tries and kicking 14 penalties also played soccer for Gloucester City, for during the 1929-30 season he played left back for the City club.

POSTPONED

The Gloucester Rugby versus Newcastle Falcons Guinness Premiership match on 22nd December 2006 was postponed due to fog by referee Rob Debney within minutes of the kick off. The crowd were in the Kingsholm ground to no avail. Within an hour of the postponement the game could have been played. Vision was possible the length and breadth of Kingsholm!

FIVE AT THE TOP

There are five players who have made a total of over 500 first team appearances for the Club – Alan Brinn, Peter Ford, Bob Clewes, Richard Mogg and Dick Smith.

PHILIPPE'S RECORD AS DIRECTOR OF COACHING

The popular Frenchman won more matches than he lost in his reign at Kingsholm 1998 to 2002.

HOME MATCHES					
Played	Won	Drew	Lost	Points For	Points Against
51	40	1	10	1658	902

AWAY MATCHES					
Played	Won	Drew	Lost	Points For	Points Against
49	20	1	28	1159	1203

OVERALL RECORD					
Played	Won	Drew	Lost	Points For	Points Against
100	60	2	38	2,817	2,105

POINTS EVOLUTION

There have been many alterations to the value of point scoring in the game of Rugby Union since its origin.

YEARS	TRY	CONVERSIONS	PENALTIES	DROPPED GOAL
1891	1	2	2	3
1892-1893	2	3	3	4
1894-1895	3	2	3	4
1896-1947	3	2	3	3
1948-1971	3	2	3	3
1972-1991	4	2	3	3
1992	5	2	3	3

POLICEMAN

John Fidler is one of eighteen England Internationals who have served as Policemen in the community.

PUBLIC ADDRESS

The public address system was installed at Kingsholm in 1950. Up to that year pre-match entertainment had been provided by the Cinderford Town band.

POPULATION

The population of the City of Gloucester reached 39,444 in 1892.

PROFESSIONAL IN THE NORTH

In 1894 the clubs from the North of England split from the Rugby Football Union to form a professional game. In the process they attracted players from Gloucester.

PITCH

The pitch was repositioned in 1900 to enable spectators to have a better view from the newly build grandstand.

PILKINGTON CUP

The 'Cherry and Whites' were semi-finalists in the R.F.U. National Cup in 1984-85, 1988-89, 1991-92, 1995-96, 1996-97, 1998-99, 2008-09.

PLAYERS LURED

Players were lured away to other clubs in 1991 at the end of the season including England International, Mike Teague to Moseley. In all 15 players left the Club. Gloucester were trying to retain its amateur ethos.

PLAYERS IN CRISIS

Players called a crisis meeting with the Club Coach in 1992 with regard to the lack of player rewards compared with other clubs.

PHILIPPE – THE FIRST

Philippe St Andre, the former Gloucester Rugby Club Director of Coaching became the first wing three-quarter in 1994 to captain France for 27 years, the first since Christian Darroway captained the French team.

PHILIPPE

Philippe St Andre, the former French International was the first coach to lead Gloucester into the Heineken Cup. He was also the Club's first overseas player in the professional era.

ENGLAND NEEDED A 'P'

Four players with their name commencing with the letter 'P' have played for England – Graham Parker, Henry Paul, Malcolm Preedy and Tom Price.

ALL THE P's

Opponents have been: Padova, Paris St Francais, Penylan, Percy Park, Penzance, Philadelphia University, Perpignan, Pill Harriers, Plymouth Albion, Pontypool, Pontypridd, Portugal, Presidents XV, Public School Wanderers, Penarth, Penycraig and Plymouth.

PAUL IN TANDEM

Henry Paul had the rare distinction of playing Rugby League for New Zealand and Rugby Union for England.

LOWEST POINTS

The lowest points recorded in a season were 140 in the 1895/96 campaign. Only 10 points came from ten away fixtures.

PATERSON THE YOUNGER

Chris Paterson is the youngest player to reach 50 caps for Scotland. He was 26 years of age when he reached this milestone versus South Africa at Murrayfield, Edinburgh in November 2004.

POTTING THEM ALL

Chris Paterson kicked a record 19 consecutive successful kicks at goal in the 2007 Six Nations Championship; this was after missing his first kick in the first match of that season against England at Twickenham.

PAUL ONE OF 140

Henry Paul gained 23 caps for New Zealand at Rugby League and after joining Gloucester Rugby Club was capped 6 times at England at Rugby Union. Henry is one of 140 players who have gained caps for England but were not born in England.

POINTS AVERAGE

Former Gloucester full back, Grahame Parker is among the players who have averaged more than 5 points per cap for England, averaging 12 points per match. Grahame played in the Calcutta Cup match at Twickenham on 19 March 1938 when the BBC broadcast live pictures of that game. Although there were reported to be just seventeen television sets in the whole of Britain at that time.

LEADING POINT SCORERS IN ALL MATCHES

Peter Butler	2,961
Eric Stephens	1,562

Tim Smith	1,277
Mark Mapletoft	1,265
Harold Boughton	1,240
Ludovic Mercier	1,224
Bob Clewes	1,027
Arthur Hudson	943
George Romans	801
Tom Millington	725
Paul Ford	602
Richard Mogg	593
G. James	561
Charles Smith	554
Don Rutherford	542
Malcom Baker	535
Henry Paul	283

PENCE

The European Challenge Cup programme versus London Irish in May 2006 cost £4.00.

The Pilkington Cup Final programme versus Bath at Twickenham in May 1990 cost £1.

A Gloucester versus Cambridge University programme in January 1975 cost 5 pence.

A Gloucester versus Oxford University programme in October 1983 cost 20 pence.

A Gloucester versus Sale programme in September 2008 cost £3.

The E.D.F. Energy Cup semi final programme in March 2009 cost £4.

The E.D.F. Energy Cup final programme in April 2009 cost £5.

PROFESSIONALISM

Since the advent of the professional game in a 12-year span Gloucester have had a total of nine officially appointed captains.

POINTS

The highest number of points reached in a Premiership season was the 82 points gained in the season of 2002-03 when seventeen matches were won, two drawn and just three lost. Seven try bonus points were gained and three losing bonus points. South African born Jake Boer was the Club Captain that season. The seventeen victories is the highest total of wins in a season since League matches were introduced.

PAYMENT

When the game of Rugby Union went open in May 1996, clubs were given a sum of £500,000 from the R.F.U. at the beginning of the following season. That sum has risen to £1.8 million and then the current £4.4 million. The £1.8 million salary cap was introduced for the beginning of the 1999/2000 season. An attempt to raise to £4.4 million was originally rejected in 2007.

POINTS

In the 2006/07 season Gloucester scored 397 points in the first half of their matches and 464 in the second half. They conceded 373 in the first half and 314 in the second half.

TOM PRICE

Former Gloucester, Cheltenham and England prop forward Tom Price had a close in Cheltenham named after him in February 1983 – Tom Price Close. Tom appeared in all the unofficial Internationals for England in 1945-46. Tom Price retired in 1937 after suffering a head injury; however he returned within 12 months and went onto play for England after the Second World War.

POOR DISPLAY

On 5th May 1990 Gloucester met Bath in the Pilkington Cup Final and suffered a heavy defeat by 48 points to six at Twickenham.

PROGRAMME COSTS

A Club programme cost £1.00 in 1994; in 1992 it cost 80 pence. For the first European Cup fixture played at Kingsholm on 12th October 1996 the match day programme cost £2.00. For the Heineken Cup Semi-Final match versus

Leicester Tigers at Vicarage Road, Watford on 21st April 2001 the cost of a programme was £2.50. The Zurich Championship Final programme versus Bristol Shoguns on 8th June 2002 cost £4.00.

The Zurich Premiership Final programme with London Wasps on 31st May 2003 cost £4.00. In 1973 the Club's Centenary Year, the programme cost 3p. The John Player Cup Final programme versus Moseley cost 40 pence. The Pilkington Cup Semi-Final programme of 1989 cost 30 pence.

NATIONAL CUP WINNERS – P

Tom Palmer	1972
Mike Potter	1972
Malcolm Preedy	1982
Roy Pritchard	1982
Roy Parsloe	1982
Henry Paul	2003
Ed Pearce	2003
Junior Paramore	2003

MOST POINTS

The most points scored in a season was 1,253 in the 1991-92 season.

CHRIS PATERSON

Chris Paterson, the former Gloucester Rugby utility player had 88 International caps for Scotland and is the country's most capped player at the end of the 2007/08 season. He had scored 687 points in a career stretching from 1999. Chris made 42 consecutive appearances for his country from 2004-2008. He holds the national record for most conversions in a match with 11 versus Japan, in Perth in 2004, a match in which he totalled 44 points. Chris, has recorded 22 tries for Scotland and kicked 83 conversions, and 135 penalties. Between 2000-2008 the utility back scored 316 points for Scotland. That total included 65 in 2007 the most points in a season. Records abound for Chris as he holds the national record of 28 conversions between 2000-2008. In 2007 he kicked 16 penalties in that season of 2006-07 he kicked 7 penalties versus Wales for Scotland.

Q

QUERA

Akapusi Quera became the ninth player to record a hat trick of tries in League matches in the professional era.

Akapusi of course registered his hat trick of tries versus Leeds on 19th April 2008. The second hat trick by a Gloucester player versus Leeds in the same season of 2007-2008.

Akapusi Quera was the first Fijian International to play for Gloucester when he signed a contract in 2007.

QUEEN VICTORIA

Queen Victoria who died at Osborne House on the Isle of Wight on 22nd January 1901 was honoured by both Ireland and England on 9th February when the teams paid their respect. Included in the England team was Charles Hall of Gloucester Rugby Club. A match England lost by 10 points to six at Twickenham.

QUENTIN DAVIDS

There were high hopes that former Stormers and Western Province lock forward Quentin Davids from South Africa would be a force to be reckoned with when he joined the Club in 2004 but he proved unable to stake a claim to a position in the team and he returned to his native land at the latter end of 2005/06 season.

OTHER Q's

When Akapusi Quera signed for Gloucester Rugby Club in 2007 it was widely thought that no other players with a surname commencing with the letter Q had played for the Club previous. In actual fact two players had done so, oddly with the same surname. F. E. Quixley made three 1st XV appearances in 1910 and H. Quixley made 54 first team appearances from 1904 to 1907.

QUEUES

Queues began to form at 10.30 a.m. for the 1940 England versus Wales wartime International at Kingsholm on 13 April 1940. Over 100 police were drafted into the City to deal with the crowd as well as 60 special constables. There were 15,000 tickets on sale.

A QUIZZICAL TIME

Gloucester R.F.C. competed in the Rothmans Rugby Quiz Tournament in 1978. It was a tournament based on the contents of the Rothmans Rugby Yearbook. In the first round of the tournament they faced a local derby when they were drawn away to nearby Cheltenham.

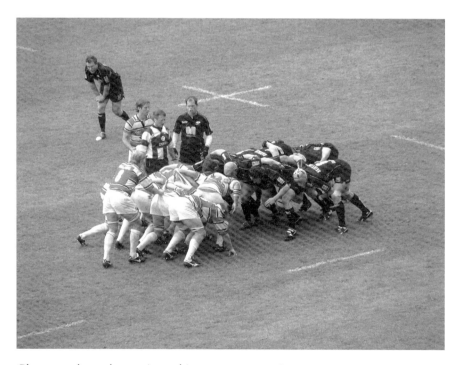

Gloucester have the put-in at this 2005 game against saracens

R

RYAN ON THE SABBATH

Gloucester Rugby Club Head Coach Dean Ryan played in the first Five Nations match to be played on a Sunday when England met Scotland at Murrayfield on 22nd March 1998. A match that England won 34-20.

ROTHMANS

Rothmans Rugby Yearbook of 1995-96 named former Gloucester R.F.C. player and Director of Rugby – Philippe Saint-Andre as one of their five players of the year. Philippe, born at Romans-sur-Isere in France was born on 19th April 1967 and was playing for Montferrand at the time.

RECORDS

It is always difficult to define the playing records of the Club in the 1880s for they would have recorded fixtures against 'Next XV' or Next XX. If Gloucester won the trial match then the result was included in the playing record. If the Next team won the match then the match never statistically took place!

RECORDED

The Club recorded its 2,500th win in its history when Newport were defeated at Kingsholm on 5th February 1993. It was the Club's 4,059th match since the Club was formed by Francis Hartley.

R.F.U. AWARDS

In the 1996-97 season two players from Gloucester R.F.C. were award winners granted by the Rugby Football Union. They were:

Young Player of the Season   Phil Greening
Unisys Top Scorer   Mark Mapletoft

R.F.U. NATIONAL CUP

During the history of the National Cup one former Gloucester player collected a Runners-Up medal with two clubs! He was Kevin Dunn (Gloucester and Wasps). A former Gloucester prop forward claimed two winners' medals for two clubs – Roger Cowling (Gloucester and Leicester).

THE FIRST

Don Rutherford, the former Gloucester and England full back became the Rugby Football Union's first professional Technical Director in 1969. He remained in this post for 30 years. Don now lives near Penzance in Cornwall.

WAY UP NORTH

The Rugby League records of the players who represented Gloucester Rugby Football Club and then defected to Rugby League are as follows:

Billy Hall – Oldham R.L.F.C. 1913-1925 made 240 appearances, scoring 53 tries, kicked 2 goals and totalled 163 points with the Northern club. Billy Hall was the youngest of seven rugby playing brothers and was born in Gloucester. A centre or standoff he moved to Coventry R.F.C. before joining Oldham R.L.F.C. He made 138 appearances for Gloucester R.F.C. scoring 31 tries, adding three conversions and 4 drop goals.

Dave Holland – Oldham R.L.F.C. 1913-1921 made 87 appearances, scoring 19 tries, totalling 57 points. David Holland (1906-1909) played for Gloucester R.F.C. and Devonport Albion. It was from the Devon club he moved north to join Oldham R.L.F.C.

Alf Wood – Oldham R.L.F.C. – 1908-1920. On his Rugby League debut Alfred kicked seven goals in a 38-0 victory. In his first season with the Club he kicked 71 goals. Alf made 244 appearances for Oldham kicking 342 goals to total 684 points. He was a member of the Oldham team that defeated Wigan 13-7 in the 1910 League Championship Final. He also played soccer for Oldham Athletic.

Ken Wilson – Oldham R.L.F.C. 1963-1973. Ken made 321 appearances (including 5 as a substitute for the Rugby League club scoring 25 tries, 6 goals and totalled 87 points. He was appointed the Club Coach in 1971.

REDPATH

Gloucester coach and former Scotland International scrum half Bryan Redpath represented South of Scotland at cricket and athletics. Bryan's brother Craig played for Scotland Under 21s and 'B' team at Rugby Union and his sister Lynne for Scotland Women's Under 21s. Bryan made 60 International appearances for Scotland between 1993 and 2003.

RUTHERFORD

Former Gloucester and England full back Don Rutherford was in the England XV that faced Wales in the first Five Nations match of 1960. That same XV played in all four England matches that season. Yet seven players were making their debut versus Wales including Don who was then a member of Percy Park R.F.C. The England side, for the first time in its history was unchanged throughout the season.

DEAN RYAN

Former Gloucester Rugby Head Coach, Dean Ryan, gained four caps for England but never appeared at Twickenham for his country.

THOMAS ROBINSON

The first match played at Kingsholm was kicked off by the Mayor of Gloucester, Thomas Robinson. He was later to become the City Member of Parliament and eventually knighted.

RELATIONS

Relations among players had always been prominent in the history of the Club. There have been 28 sets of brothers and eight father and son combinations.

REVENUE – LOSS

In 1996 the Revenue from Hospitality boxes and sponsorship dropped dramatically.

RED & WHITES

The club was referred to as the 'Red and Whites' well into the 1960s.

ONLY 2 R's

Donald Rutherford and Peter Richards are the only players with their surname commencing with the letter 'R' to have played for England.

ALL THE R's

Opponents have been: Redruth, Rest of County, Richmond, Rockliffe, Rosslyn Park, Rotherham, Roma, Roundhay, Royal Artillery Cadet, Royal Navy, Royal Tank Corps, Rugby, Runcorn, Royal Air Force, Richmond, Redland Park and Rocklease.

GEORGE ROMANS

George Romans holds the Club record for the most conversions kicked in a match – eleven versus Clifton in 1901.

REDPATH ON RIGHT PATH

Bryan Redpath, the Gloucester Rugby Club Coach is the most capped Scotland International in the scrum half position having been awarded 60 caps.

RAIDING THE NORTHERN GAME

Gloucester Rugby Club have headed north on three occasions to tempt players from Rugby League and convert to Rugby Union. All three players have been recruited from Bradford Bulldogs – Henry Paul, Karl Pryce and Lesley Vainikolo.

RUGBY WORLD CUP MATCH

Kingsholm staged a Pool 1 World Cup match on Tuesday 8th October 1991 when New Zealand met United States of America. The price of the match day programme was £1.50. Included in the All Blacks squad was lock forward Ian Jones who was to later join Gloucester Rugby Club.

REFEREE

How the personnel now officiating in the Premier League have changed since the inaugural season 1996-97 when the game of Rugby Union became professional. Our first home match that season was against Sale at Kingsholm on 7th September 1996 in Courage League One. The result was a victory for our Northern visitors by 16 points to twelve. The referee was Tony Spreadbury. Mark Mapletoft landed all our points from four penalties. The Sale points were attributed to Steve Diamond with a try, with Griffin converting. The latter also landed three penalties.

Other officials to visit Kingsholm in that inaugural season were Brian Campsall, D. Chapman, T. Rossall, Ed Morrison, Steve Lander, Ashley Rowden, Graham Hughes and John Pearson along with Chris Rees.

Our Anglo Welsh League matches were administered by C. Adams, Geoff Warren and Jim Fleming. Alan Lewis, of Ireland officiated his first European match when Begles Bordeaux came to Kingsholm on 16th October 1996. The Irish official has now refereed more European matches than any other official.

Paddy O'Brien of New Zealand was in charge of our Pilkington Cup tie with Bristol on 25th January in our 16-12 success.

S

SPA

It was a memorable day on the 2nd February 1889 when the Spa, the former home of Gloucester R.F.C. staged a match between Gloucestershire and the touring Maoris. The Spa was an open ground but for this special occasion. Permission was obtained to put canvas round the field and a gate of £193 was taken – easily a record in receipts for a football match in the City at their old headquarters. The Maoris were led by full back Joe Warbrick. Gloucester R.F.C. as the leading Club in the County provided eleven players to the Gloucestershire team. The tourists beat the County by 1 goal, 1 try to 1 try. The County top scorer was R. Grist of Gloucester R.F.C. The Maoris were engaged in 74 matches on that tour, winning 49, losing 20 and drawing 5.

A crowd of over 8,000 attended to watch the County team which was captained by H. C. Baker, the Clifton International. With eleven players from Gloucester R.F.C. there were two from Clifton and one each from the Royal Agricultural College, Cirencester and the Bristol Medicals.

SEVENS

Gloucester R.F.C. made their first serious incursion into the seven-a-side game in 1971 when they won the Tewkesbury Sevens. Their next success in this facet of the game came when they won the Ross Centenary Sevens on Sunday 30th September 1978.

SIMPSON-DANIEL

James Simpson-Daniel, the Club's utility three-quarter played in Twickenham's first Sunday International when England played Italy in the Six Nations Championship on 9th March 2003. James was one of England's try scorers in a 40 points to five victory.

SMART AT EASTER

Sydney Smart the former Gloucester forward has played for England on an Easter Monday in two of only eight matches played by England. Both were away to France in 1912 and 1914. Sydney was also a member of the first England team to lose at Twickenham when South Africa won 9-3 on 4th January 1913.

SMITH SENT OFF ON DEBUT

This was the misfortune that befell former Gloucester and Scotland flanker Ian Smith. Ian made his debut at Roehampton on Wednesday 15th September 1982 against Rosslyn Park. It was almost the final whistle when Park prop Paul Curtis was ordered off for kicking Gloucester hooker Kevin White. Ian Smith retaliated with a punch. The 'Cherry and Whites' losing by 17 points to nine.

SUSPENSIONS

In the 2002-2003 season the Club had four players suspended:

Mark Cornwell	1 match for 3 yellow cards in a 12 month period
Ed Pearce	21 days for stamping versus Wasps on 26th October 2002
Chris Fortey	12 weeks for stamping on opponent's head
Jake Boer	1 match for 3 yellow cards in a 12 month period

IAN SMITH

Ian Smith, the former Gloucester and Scotland flanker was the first Gloucester player to reach the landmark of 100 League appearances for the Club.

SUPPORTERS

It was estimated that Gloucester Rugby Club took over 20,000 supporters to the National Cup Final in 1990 and approximately 30,000 to the Final of 2003 against Northampton. On 18th April 2009 for the E.D.F. Cup Final versus Cardiff Blues there were an estimated 25,000 Gloucester supporters among the overall attendance of 55,000. These games were all played at Twickenham.

OPPONENTS – S

Sale, Salford, Saracens, Second Glosters, Sidmouth, Southend, Southern Counties, Somerset Police, South Wales Borders, South Wales Police, Spain, Stade Francaise, Stade Toulouse, Stellenbosch University, Saint Bartholomew's, St Helens, St Ives, St Lukes, St Marys, Stourbridge, Stratford-on-Avon, Stroud, St Thomas and Swansea.

SUSPENDED

Fixtures were suspended during World War One, 1914-18, and the Second World War, 1939-45.

LESLIE ERIC SAXBY

Reputed to have been the oldest player to have made his debut for England, he passed away on 26th August 1956 in High Flats, Natal, South Africa. Leslie was the 690th player to be capped for his country.

STOUT AT SOCCER

Frank Moxham Stout who attended Crypt Grammar School played soccer for Gloucester City. Such was the sporting prowess within the Stout family that brother Percy also played Rugby Union and was capped by England while their father, William Stout won the Diamond Sculls at Henley. Percy Stout was a fine soccer player with Corinthians.

SOUTH AFRICANS

The South Africans who have arrived at Kingsholm in the professional era have been:

J. Boer, D. Du Preez, R. Van Der Berg, C. Bezuienhout, T. Delport, Q. Davids and R. Kiel.

HOW MANY SMITHS ARE THERE?

Often considered by many to be the most common surname in England, well Gloucester R.F.C. can vouch for that fact for no fewer than 21 players have represented Gloucester 1st XV with that name. They are as follows:

A. Smith (1900-1901), A. Smith (1904), A. Smith (1947), C. 'Whacker' Smith (1897-1907), Frank Smith (1905-1910), G. Smith (1919-1920), George H. Smith (1897-1904), H. Smith (1911), Hubert Smith (1903-1908), J. Smith (1906), J. V. Smith (1948), K. Smith (1929-1936), L. Smith (1913), Lewis Smith (1896-1902), Bob Smith (1957-1964), Dick Smith (1958-1975), W. Smith (1896), W. Smith (1904), H. G. Smith (1952-1955), T. Smith (1982-1996), I. Smith (1983-97).

LESS OF THE STEPHENS

Not so many Stephens as Smiths but there have been seven players with that surname to have represented Gloucester 1st XV. They are as follows:

Arthur Stephens (1891-1898), E. C. Stephens (1926-1930), E. J. Stephens (1961-1973), J. Stephens (1926-1928), James Stephens (1894-1910), S. Stephens (1909), T. Stephens (1927-1939).

SCOTS

While Peter Jones and Ian Smith were Scottish Internationals, both were born in Gloucestershire. However, there have been Scots who have moved to Kingsholm from over the border:

D. Crichton-Miller, S. Brotherstone, A. Dickinson, R. Lawson, A. Strokosch, C. Paterson and S. Lawson.

LESLIE SAXBY

When Leslie Saxby was capped by England on 2nd January 1932 versus South Africa at St Helens, Swansea he was believed to have been 40 years of age. Public records indicate he was born in the Bradfield area in 1900.

PERCY STOUT

Percy Stout and Ryan Lamb are the only players to have recorded the 'full hand' for the Club. Percy in one match versus Weston-Super-Mare R.F.C. in 1898 he scored four tries, five conversions, two penalties and one dropped goal. Ryan Lamb scored a try, four conversions, one penalty and one drop goal versus Bristol at Kingsholm on 21st November 2008 in a Guinness Premiership encounter.

THE 'SPA'

The Club played their matches at 'The Spa' until the 1890/91 season.

SPECTATING

There were 4,000 spectators present at the first match played at Kingsholm on 10th October 1891 versus Burton on Trent.

SUSPENSION

The Club were suspended by the Rugby Football Union in 1895 for 'professionalism'. This was due to players being recruited by Gloucester Football Club. It was then stated that in future the Club would be adopting an extremely rigid adherence to the amateur regulations and upon this promise the Club were re-instated.

SIXPENNY STAND – THE SHED

The 'sixpenny' stand now known as the 'Shed' was opened in 1912. There was a small grandstand named St Mark's Pavilion over part of the terracing in its early days.

ALL SEALED

C. Seeling was one of three All Blacks to play for Gloucester versus Leicester in 1905 on 13th January.

TOO MANY SPECTATORS

In the 1919/20 season there were 8,000 attending the match versus Newport at Kingsholm. It raised concerns that so many spectators would cause problems in future.

SAFETY

The Safety of Sports Ground Act following the Hillsborough Football disaster required £200,000 worth of safety measures to be completed in 1986.

SECOND

In the 1988/89 season the Club were second in the Courage League Cup.

SIMMO – THE FIRST

David Sims, the Club Captain became Gloucestershire Rugby Football Clubs first full time professional in May 1996 signing a two-year contract.

SPECTATORS

There were 8,000 spectators present when Gloucester played Swansea at the Spa in the 1891/92 season.

EIGHT 'S'

The surnames commencing with the letter 'S' number eight who represented England:

Gordon Sargent, Les Saxby, James Simpson-Daniel, David Sims, Sidney Smart, Charles Smith, Frank and Percy Stout.

ALL THE S's

Opponents have been: Sale, Salford, Saracens, Second Glosters, Sidmouth, Southend, Southern Counties, Somerset Police, South Wales Borders, South

Wales Police, Spain, Stade Francais, Stade Toulouse, Stellenbosch University, St Bartholomews, St Helens, St Ives, St Lukes, St Marys, Stourbridge, Stratford-on-Avon, Stroud, St Thomas and Swansea.

CHARLES SMITH

Charles Smith holds the record for the most tries in a match when he scored eight versus Clifton in 1901.

STOUT IN NATURE

Frank and Percy Stout appeared in England's victory on 2nd April 1898 at Blackheath. It was to be England's last victory over the Principality for 12 years. England winning by 14 points to seven, both Percy and Frank recording tries!

SMART MOVE

Sydney Smart of Gloucester Rugby Football Club played in all of the England's matches when they won the Triple Crown, Championship of the Five Nations as well as the Grand Slam in 1914.

SCOTLAND CAPS

There have been seven players from Gloucester Rugby Club capped by Scotland: Donald Crighton-Miller, Ian Smith, Peter Jones, Alistair Strokosch, Alistair Dickenson, Chris Paterson and Rory Lawson.

SAMOA

Both Terry Fanolua and Junior Paramore were capped by the Southern Hemisphere country whilst they were players with the Kingsholm club.

DAVID SIMS

Dave Sims, Gloucester born and the Club's first professional made 130 league appearances and eight as a replacement scoring a total of 43 points.

SECOND CENTURY

In the Pilkington Cup Final of 1990, Ian Smith the Cherry and White flanker made his 200th appearance for the Club.

SIZE

The size of the Premier League in Rugby Union saw a top division of ten clubs in 1995/96. It rose to twelve clubs for one season in 1998/99 it was increased again to fourteen clubs which enabled each club to play 26 league matches. The format then returned to twelve clubs.

SHEDHEAD FANZINE

The Shedhead fanzine was founded in 1995 by authors Bob Fenton and Ed Snow. A magazine for supporters to voice an opinion of their Club.

SOUND OF MUSIC

Gloucester supporters are the country's biggest music lovers among premiership clubs, averaging £31 per month at music stores!

STRONGMAN

Alasdair Strokosch, the Gloucester flanker was a karate black belt by the age of 12.

NATIONAL CUP WINNERS – S

Gordon Sargent	1978
John Simonett	1978
James Simpson-Daniel	2003
Eric Stephens	1972
Dick Smith	1972

SQUADS

Over the various seasons since the advent of professionalism the squad of players that have represented the 'Cherry and Whites' have changed dramatically. Those players who have played in League fixtures season by season are:

1996-97   P. Hart, C. Catling, A. Lumsden, M. Lloyd, E. Anderson, D. Timmington, P. Holford, M. Peters, D. Caskie, A. Saverimutto, C. Emmerson, L. Osborne, M. Roberts, M. Kimber, M. Mapletoft, C. Mulraine, S. Benton, L. Beck, A. Powles, T. Windo, J. Hawker, P. Greening, C. Fortey, P. Vickery, A. Deacon, R. Ward, R. Fidler, D. Sims, S. Devereaux, R. York, P. Glanville, A. Stanley, E. Pearce, I. Smith, N. Carter, D. Edwards and T. Woodman. (37 Players)

1997-98   P. St Andre, T. Windo, R. Fidler, M. Mapletoft, T. Fanolua, R. Tombs, P. Glanville, N. Osman, C. Catling, N. Carter, S. Benton, S. Devereaux, M. Cornwell, P. Vickery, D. Sims, S. Ojomoh, A. Lumsden, B. Johnson, C. Fortey, N. Mccarthy, A. Deacon, P. Greening, L. Beck, R. Jewell, R. St Andre, A. Powles, E. Pearce, C. Emmerson, I. Sanders, M. Lloyd and A. Hazell. (31 Players)

1998-99   S. Ojomoh, N. Carter, R. Tombs, T. Woodman, C. Catling, C. Fortey, M. Cornwell, D. Sims, N. Mccarthy, S. Mannix, R. Fidler, P. St. Andre, M. Mapletoft, A. Deacon, E. Pearce, T. Fanolua, S. Benton, B. Johnson, T. Windo, I. Sanders, A. Lumsden, R. Greenslade-Jones, A. Hazell, S. Devereaux, R. Ward, T. Beim, P. Vickery, A. Powles, R. Jewell, A. Eustace, M. Kimber, K. Jones, P. Greening, J. Hawkins, P. Glanville, M. Davies, I. Ward, R. Stott, A. Dawling, N. Cane and L. Beck. (41 Players)

1999-00   C. Catling, R. Tombs, B. Hayward, T. Fanolua, T. Beim, B. Johnson, J. Ewens, R. Jewell, T. Glassie, C. Yates, S. Mannix, M. Kimber, E. Moncreiff, I. Sanders, L. Beck, T. Woodman, S. Simon, A. Powles, L. Sanchez, C. Fortey, D. Djoudi, N. McCarthy, A. Deacon, P. Vickery, R. Fidler, R. Ward, A. Eustace, M. Cornwell, I. Jones, S. Ojomoh, P. Glanville, E. Pearce, K. Jones, A,Hazell, T. Micklausic, J. Paramore, D. Carr and C. Collins. (38 Players)

2000-01 A. Murray, T. Fanolua, C. Catling, R. Greenslade-Jones, J. Ewens, C. Yates, R. Jewell, S. Mannix, B. Hayward, I. Sanders, A. Powles, S. Simon, O. Azam, D. Djoudi, A. Deacon, R. Fidler, M. Cornwell, I. Jones, S. Ojomoh, A. Eustace, J. Paramore, J. Boer, G. Gregoire, F. Schisano, K. Jones, A. Gomarsall, S. Sanchez, E. Pearce, D. Lougheed, C. Fortey, A. Hazell, T. Beim, P. Vickery, J. Little, E. Moncreiff, T. Woodman, J. Simpson-Daniel, R. Todd, J. Goodridge, J. Goatley, J. Forrester and T. Miklausic. (42 Players)

2001-02 C. Catling, C. Stoica, R. Todd, D. O'Leary, H. Paul, J. Ewens, T. Fanolua, D. Albanese, J. Simpson-Daniel, J. Frape, T. Beim, L. Mercier, D. Yachvili, A. Gomarsall, P. Collazo, F. Pucciariello, T. Woodman, P. Vickery, A. Deacon, C. Fortey, O. Azam, R. Fidler, M. Cornwell, A. Eustace, E. Pearce, J. Boer, J. Forrester, K. Sewabu, A. Hazell, J. Paramore, J. Goodridge, M. Garvey, S. Mannix, C. Gillies and P. Calleit. (35 Players)

2002-03 T. Delport, H. Paul, C. Catling, M. Garvey, T. Beim, D. O'Leary, T. Fanolua, R. Todd, J. Simpson-Daniel, L. Mercier, S. Amor, A. Comarsall, C. Stuart-Smith, T. Woodman, P. Collazo, R. Roncero, O. Azam, C. Fortey, C. Collins, P. Vickery, A. Deacon, D. Molloy, E. Pearce, R. Fidler, A. Eustace, M. Cornwell, J. Boer, P. Buxton, A. Hazell, J. Forrester, L. Narraway, J. Paramore, R. Ellaway, A. Cave, C. Collins, A. Frost, M. Irish and S. Amor. (38 Players)

2003-04 R. Teague, J. Goodridge, T. Delport, R. Van De Berg, M. Garvey, M. Foster, T. Fanolua, R. Todd, J. Simpson-Daniel, H. Paul, G. Thomas, J. Frape, B. Davies, S. Amor, D. Mcrae, A. Page, A. Gomarsall, P. Johnstone, N. Wood, R. Roncero, T. Woodman, S. Brotherstone, C. Fortey, A. Deacon, A. Olver, P. Vickery, A. Eustace, M. Cornwell, A. Brown, J. Boer, J. Forrester, P. Buxton, A. Hazell, J. Paramore, W. Matthews, C. Collins, R. Elloway, D. Du Preez, R. Guess and A. Frost, J. Merriman. (41 Players)

2004-05 J. Goodridge, M. Garvey, T. Fanolua, H. Paul, D. McRae J. Simpson-Daniel, S. Amor, T. Sigley, O. Azam, G. Powell, A. Eustace, A. Brown, J. Boer, J. Forrester, A. Balding, N. Wood, C. Fortey, P. Buxton, M. Cornwell, A. Hazell, A. Gomarsall,

J. Bailey, S. Emms, P. Vickery, C. Buzuidenhout, N. Mauger, B. Davies, A. Page, S. Kiole, J. Parkes, M. Davies, N. Curnier, L. Narraway, M. Foster, J. Merriman and O. Morgan. (36 Players)

2005-06   J. Goodridge, D. McRae, R. Thirlby, O. Morgan, L. Mercier, H. Thomas, M. Foster, B. Davies, T. Fanolua, R. Keil, J. Bailey, J. Simpson-Daniel, M. Tindall, J. Adams, A. Allen, H. Paul, R. Lamb, P. Richards, S. Amor, P. Collazo, G. Powell, T. Sigley, N. Wood, J. Forster, L. Narraway, O. Azam, M. Davies, J. Parkes, R. Elloway, P. Vickery, A. Eustace, Q. Davids, J. Boer, J. Pendlebury, A. Brown, P. Buxton, M. Cornwell, A. Balding, A. Hazell, J. Merriman and J. Forrester. (41 Players)

2006-07   O. Morgan, I. Balshaw, W. Walker, J. Adams, J. Bailey, R. Keil, J. Simpson-Daniel, L. Narraway, M. Tindall, A. Allen, J. Boer, M. Foster, K. Pryce, B. Davies, L. Mercier, R. Lamb, C. Nieto, J. Goodridge, P. Richards, R. Lawson, H. Thomas, N. Wood, J. Forster, P. Collazo, C. Califano, M. Davies, O. Azam, R. Elloway, M. Bortolami, W. James, A. Eustace, A,Brown, J. Pendlebury, P. Buxton, A. Hazell, J. Forrester and A. Balding. (37 Players)

2007-08   I. Balshaw, O. Morgan, W. Walker, M. Foster, L. Lloyd, J. Simpson-Daniel, C. Paterson, C. Sharples, R. Lamb, M. Tindall, A. Qera, J. Adams, A. James, H. Trinder, N. Wood, L. Vainikolo, D. Norton, M. Prendergast, D. Lewis, G. Cooper, R. Lawson, P. Collazo, C. Califano, A. Dickinson, O. Azam, A. Titterell, J. Paul, C. Nieto, J. Forster, J. Pendlebury, A. Strokosch, P. Buxton, W. James, M. Bortolami, A. Qera L. Narraway, P. Buxton, D. Tuohy, A. Brown, G. Delve, A. Hazell and A. Balding. (42 Players)

2008-09   O. Morgan, I. Balshaw, L. Vainikolo, W. Walker, R. Lamb, M. Watkins, J. Simpson-Daniel, M. Tindall, M. Foster, O. Satala, H. Trinder, C. Sharples, A. Allen, O. Barkley, C. Spencer, R. Lawson, G. Cooper, D. Lewis, D. Young, N. Wood, J. Pasqualin, A. Dickinson, A. Titterell, O. Azam, S. Lawson, C. Nieto, J. Forster, G. Somerville, M. Bortolami, W. James, A. Eustace, A. Brown, A. Strokosch, P. Buxton, A. Hazell, L. Narraway, G. Delve, C. Sharples, H. Trinder and D. Williams. (40 Players)

SIMPSON-DANIEL

At the completion of the 2008-09 season James Simpson-Daniel had scored 44 tries in League matches. James, is not only the 'Cherry and Whites', top try scorer since Leagues were formed but also since the advent of professional rugby union.

James record reads as follows season by season.

Season	Opposition	Venue	Date	Result	Tries
2000-01	Rotherham	Home	10th March	Won 50-17	1

	Opposition	Venue	Date	Result	Tries
	Bristol	Home	10th November	Won 51-17	1
Season	Leeds	Home	1st December	Won 58-17	2
2001-02	Sale	Home	9th March	Won 42-14	1
	Bath	Home	4th May	Won 68-12	3
	Leeds	Away	12th May	Won 50-17	2

Season	Opposition	Venue	Date	Result	Tries
2002-03	Harlequins	Home	26th April	Won 29-11	1

	Opposition	Venue	Date	Result	Tries
	Saracens	Home	27th September	Won 30-7	1
	Newcastle	Away	5th October	Lost 22-42	1
Season	Leeds	Home	25th October	Won 24-19	2
2003-04	Northampton	Home	29th November	Won 28-20	1
	Harlequins	Home	27th December	Won 18-17	1
	London Irish	Home	18th April	Won 30-10	1
	Wasps	Home	1st May	Won 28-25	1

	Opposition	Venue	Date	Result	Tries
Season	Leeds	Away	5th September	Won 21-16	1
2004-05	Newcastle	Home	25th September	Won 31-17	1
	Harlequins	Home	9th October	Won 29-23	1

	Opposition	Venue	Date	Result	Tries
Season 2005-06	Northampton	Home	24th September	Won 28-24	1
	Leeds	Home	31st December	Won 31-7	2
	Bristol	Home	25th March	Lost 15-20	1
	Worcester	Home	15th April	Won 27-16	1
	Leeds	Away	30th April	Won 31-7	1

	Opposition	Venue	Date	Result	Tries
Season 2006-07	London Irish	Away	10th November	Won 22-11	1
	Sale	Away	6th January	Lost 19-20	1
	Northampton	Away	3rd March	Won 7-5	1

	Opposition	Venue	Date	Result	Tries
Season 2007-08	Leeds	Away	16th September	Won 49-24	1
	Worcester	Home	29th September	Won 29-7	1
	Bristol	Home	29th December	Won 27-0	1
	Bristol	Away	16th February	Lost 26-29	1
	Newcastle	Home	23rd February	Won 28-20	1
	Harlequins	Home	1st March	Lost 25-30	1
	Saracens	Home	12th March	Won 39-15	1
	Wasps	Away	4th May	Won 25-17	1
	Bath	Home	10th May	Won 8-6	1

	Opposition	Venue	Date	Result	Tries
Season 2008-09	Newcastle	Home	30th September	Won 39-23	2
	Bath	Home	28th February	Won 36-27	2

Of the current Guinness Premiership clubs the only club that James Simpson-Daniel has not scored against in a league match is Leicester Tigers!

T

TEAGUE AWAY FROM KINGSHOLM

Mike Teague played his first match for Moseley against Wasps on 5th September 1992 and played for the Midland Club for two seasons before returning to Kingsholm for a final swansong. Whilst with Moseley he played for England against South Africa in 1992 and also in the International Championship against France, Wales, Scotland and Ireland in 1993.

He was in the 1993 British Lions partly that toured New Zealand. Mike appeared in seven matches (non tests) and in the 2nd Test Match when he came on as a blood replacement but did not appear in any of the other Test matches.

At that time Moseley were members of the National Division 2.

THE TUMP

Arose when the Kingsholm pitch was first laid in 1891. The clearing of the ground in preparation saw the soil created and deposited at the far end from Worcester Street and therefore an artificial tump was created. This allowed spectators to stand there for what was regarded as a better view. It must be remembered that the playing pitch ran at 90 to what was regarded as 'The Tump', it actually ran alongside what was the Deans Walk touchline in those early days.

TALENTED

Former Gloucester forward Alan Townsend who captained the Club in the 1961-62 season and in a career that stretched from 1956 to 1964 in which he made 191 first team appearances scoring 5 tries has a grandson Jose who graduated from Central Saint Martin's Art College, London in 2006. He had produced portraits of not only Allan but also of All Black legend Colin Meads and England International soccer player Rio Ferdinand.

TITTERELL

Former Gloucester Rugby Club hooker Andy Titterell holds the record for having the most caps as a replacement, four, without starting a match for England.

'KIT'

Christopher 'Kit' Tanner, the former Club three quarter was one of 14 England International players who died in the Second World War.

TEAM TRIES SCORED IN PROFESSIONAL ERA – LEAGUE

1995-1996	20
1996-1997	46
1997-1998	52
1998-1999	58
1999-2000	68
2000-2001	43
2001-2002	68
2002-2003	67
2003-2004	51
2004-2005	43
2005-2006	41
2006-2007	50
2007-2008	50
2008-2009	43

TOP TRY

When a club record of 1,145 points were recorded in the season of 1972/73 a club record of 161 tries were scored.

TOURISTS

Touring teams that have appeared at Kingsholm:

a)   The All Blacks of 1905-06 inflicted a heavy defeat on the 'City' as the Club were then known by 44 points to nil.

b)   The Australians of 1st October 1908 defeated Gloucestershire 16
      points to nil.

c)   The All Blacks of 1924-25 attracted an attendance in excess of
      12,000 to Kingsholm. Gate receipts realised £1,300. They defeated
      the County by six points to nil.

d)   On 3rd November 1906 South Africa defeated the County team by 23
      points to nil.

TOUCH JUDGES

When the Kingsholm ground hosted Burton in the opening match played there
on 10th October 1891, the two touch judges were T. G. Smith and T. E. Lovell.

A TRIO OF VICARS

Gloucester Rugby Club once fielded three vicars in the same team – Bill
Phillips, Mervyn Hughes and Chris Tanner.

NOT TOP

Mike Teague was one of 29 players to have been capped by England while
representing a club outside the top division. Mike was awarded 5 caps (1992-
93) when he played for Moseley.

'TUG'

The late Ken ('Tug') Wilson who made his one appearance for England versus
France at Twickenham on 23rd February was a Physical Training Officer in the
Royal Air Force at Innsworth at the time. 'Tug' was a prominent figure in the
boxing ring where he once defeated the famous British heavyweight Billy Walker.

TAILORED TO RUN

Walter Taylor, the Club's former wing three-quarter who also represented
the County was one of the fastest three-quarters in the country. Walter was
a Midland Counties champion who won numerous sprint races and took
part in the A.A.A. Championships. Walter played for the Club (1891-1904)

making 237 first team appearances scoring 114 tries, landing 10 conversions, a penalty goal and nine dropped goals.

DOUBTING THOMAS

Few would doubt that the surname of Thomas figures prominently in the playing statistics of this Club. Those who have made progress to the first XV are as follows:

B. A. Thomas (1967), C. P. C. Thomas (1947-1960), E. Thomas (1913), F. Thomas (1934), G. Thomas (1919-1928), H. A. Thomas (1893), H. G. Thomas (1911), J. Thomas (1935), J. Thomas (1949), K. Thomas (1958), W. Thomas (1931), W. G. Thomas (1945), G. Thomas (2002), H. Thomas (2005). Fourteen in total.

RETURN FROM TOULOUSE

A large crowd welcomed the 'City' team at the G.W.R. station on Thursday March 2nd 1911 after their return from Toulouse where they had recorded an 18points to 13 victory. Holford and Hall had scored tries and Cook added the points with a fine kicking display.

TORCH BEARER

The first International player to play for the Club was William Yiend who was born in 1861 in Winchcombe. He was the 208th player to be capped by England and made his debut at International level versus New Zealand Natives at Blackheath. He made 6 International appearances. He joined the Club from Hartlepool Rovers. William had previously played for Leicester Victoria. Upon leaving Gloucester he played for Leicester, Keighley and Peterborough. He passed away on 22nd January 1939 in Cheltenham.

TEAGUE

Gloucester Rugby Football Club legend Mike Teague made 292 appearances for the Cherry and Whites, his final match for the Club was against Harlequins at Kingsholm on 29th April at the completion of the 1994-1995 season.

'TINS'

Mike Tindall, the Gloucester Rugby Club centre three quarter lost 2 pints of blood following his freak injury against Wales in the 2008 Six Nations Championship.

NATIONAL CUP WINNERS

Paul Taylor	1972
Mike Teague	1972
Robert Todd	2003

LEADING TRY SCORERS

Since the game of Rugby Union turned professional no player has managed to score more than 9 tries in a season in League fixtures:

Chris Catling	1999-2000 – 9
Junior Paramore	2001-2002 – 9
James Simpson-Daniel	2001-2002 – 9
Jake Boer	2002-2003 – 9

TAYLOR MADE

There have been thirteen players with the surname of Taylor who have made their debuts at first team level for Gloucester R.F.C. They are as follows:

D. Taylor (1952), Dr C. C. Taylor (1924-26), H. Taylor (1903-1904), J. E. Taylor (1951-1963), K. Taylor (1960-1965), P. C. Taylor (1928), R. Taylor (1950), T. Taylor (1891), T. Taylor (1920), T. Taylor (1922), T. Taylor (1953), Walter Taylor (1891-1904) and P. Taylor.

TEAGUE – BIRTHDAY BOY

Mike Teague is one of only 17 players who have played for England on their birthday. Mike appearing for his country on 8th October 1991 versus Italy at Twickenham.

TEAGUE – WORLD CUP FIRST

Mike Teague was the first player from Gloucester Rugby Football Club to play in a World Cup match. It was in the 1991 tournament on 3rd October at Twickenham versus New Zealand in a Pool 1 match. England were defeated by 18 points to twelve.

THESIS

A thesis was written on the Club titled 'Civilising of Gloucester Rugby Football Club' by Andrew Robert White in 2000 for his PhD. There were 493 pages in four volumes.

TRY TIME

The first try credited to a player at Kingsholm was scored by Albert Henshaw in the opening match versus Burton-on-Trent in a 18 points to nil victory.

MOST TRIES

The club record for the most tries scored in a match is the 18 recorded versus Clifton in 1901.

CENTURY OF TRY SCORERS

Bob Clewes and Arthur Hudson are the only players to have recorded over one hundred points in a season solely from try scoring.

TRAINERS

The first record of the Club appointing 'trainers' came in the 1888/89 season.

TRADING LOSS

A trading loss of over £6,000 was incurred in 1977.

THE TUMP

The 'Tump' end of the Kingsholm Stadium saw fourteen hospitality boxes and new concrete terracing added in 1990.

A TRIO

Three players with the surname beginning with 'T' have played for England: Chris Tanner, Mike Teague and Mike Tindall.

ALL THE T'

Opponents have been: Tarunaki, Teignmouth, Torquay, Transsvaal, Treherbert, Trecorchy, Troedyrhi, Truro, Toulon, Tydsley and Treviso.

A TRIO AT TWICKERS

Three Gloucester players played in the first International to be played at Twickenham on 15 January 1910. They were David 'Dai' Gent, William Johns and Harold Berry.

TEAGUE

Mike Teague was a member of the England team that remained unchanged for the Five Nations season of 1991. In the same year he became the first Gloucester Rugby Football Club player to participate in a Rugby World Cup tournament. Mike played in five of England's six matches as they reached the World Cup Final. They were defeated by Australia by 12 points to six on 2nd November 1991 at Twickenham.

TINDALL – ONE OF SIX

Mike Tindall is one of six players who have scored tries against each of England's Six Nations opponents.

LEADING TRY SCORER IN PROFESSIONAL ERA (LEAGUE MATCHES)

1996-97	Mike Lloyd	7	2004-05	Terry Fanolua	6
1997-98	Terry Fanolua	8		Marcel Garvey	6
1998-99	Chris Catling	8	2005-06	Peter Richards	6
	Philippe St Andre	8	2006-07	James Bailey	5
1999-00	Chris Catling	9	2006-07	James Forrester	5
2000-01	Jason Little	6	2007-08	Lesley Vainikolo	9
2001-02	Junior Paramore	9	2007-08	James Simpson-Daniel	9
	James Simpson-Daniel	9	2007-08	James Simpson-Daniel	9
2002-03	Jake Boer	9	2008-09	Iain Balshaw	7
2003-04	James Simpson-Daniel	8		Olly Morgan	7

MIKE TINDALL

Mike Tindall, reached his 57th International cap for England (his other four were as a replacement) with eleven different partners. He started 21 times with the now retired Will Greenwood. His former Bath R.F.C. colleague Mike Catt, now of London Irish partnered Mike on 12 occasions. His other partners have been Jamie Noon (Newcastle Falcons) seven, Riki Flutey (Wasps) four, Henry Paul (Gloucester) three, Andy Farrell (Saracens) three, Stuart Abbott (London Irish) two. Other players who have made a single appearance alongside Mike are Ollie Smith (Leicester), James Simpson-Daniel (Gloucester), Toby Flood (then of Newcastle Falcons) and Olly Barkley (then of Bath R.F.C.).

TRAINING

Gloucester Rugby Club, like most clubs, once did their training at the ground itself on the actual pitch. However, clubs began to think of conserving the pitch and base their training elsewhere and also play the Club's minor matches elsewhere.

The United team for many seasons played at Kingsholm and sporadically at Oxstalls. The eventual move to Hartpury College on the North West outskirts of the City saw the Club in co-ordination with the College, whereby facilities were regarded to be some of the finest in the country. There is an all weather surface available, a gym and all the modern conveniences. If Kingsholm is unavailable due to weather conditions or purely to conserve the playing surface the Club's minor matches are staged at the College. The Club's academy is also based there too.

TWICKENHAM RECORD

1972	Moseley (R.F.U. National Cup)	10,500	Won 17-6
	Tries:	Dix, Morris.	
	Penalty:	Stephens	
	Drop Goal:	Palmer, Booth	
1978	Leicester (R.F.U. National Cup)	24,000	Won 6-3
	Try:	Mogg	
	Conversion:	Butler	
1982	Moseley (R.F.U. National Cup)	20,000	Drew 12-12
	Penalty:	Ford (4)	(extra time)
1990	Bath (R.F.U. National Cup)	52,000	Lost 6-48
	Try:	Dunn	
	Conversion:	T. Smith	
2002	Bristol (Zurich Championship Play-Off)	28,500	Won 28-23
	Try:	Boer	
	Conversion:	Mercier	
	Penalty:	Mercier (7)	
2003	Northampton (R.F.U. National Cup)	75,000	Won 40-22
	Tries:	Simpson-Daniel (2)	
		Garvey, Forrester	
	Conversion:	Mercier (4)	
	Penalty:	Mercier (3)	
	Drop Goal:	Mercier	
2003	Wasps (Zurich Championship Final)	44,000	Lost 3-39
	Penalty:	Mercier	
2005	Saracens (Zurich Wildcard)	65,000	Lost 16-24
	Tries:	B. Davies, Eustace	
	Penalty:	McRae (2)	

2007	Leicester (R.F.U. National Cup)	59,400	Lost 16-44
	Try:	Lamb	
	Conversion:	Walker	
	Penalty:	Walker (3)	

2009	Cardiff (E.D.F. Energy Cup)	55,000	Lost 12-50
	Tries:	Foster, Penalty Try	
	Conversion:	Barkley	

Gloucester glory

MARK MAPLETOFT was the toast of Kingsholm last night as he collected 18 points and his side lifted the Cheltenham and Gloucester Cup.

Coaching director Richard Hill praised his players 'guts and hard work' as they won their first trophy in 16 years, saying: "We had possibly nine first-choice players out but those that played did a fantastic job.

"They can now see something tangible after all the hard work."

And his assistant, John Brain, who has been in charge of the squad during Hill's absence with England A this week, added: "Gloucester haven't won anything meaningful in the 15-a-side format since 1982 and tonight was especially nice for the supporters."

Mapletoft went through the card and scored a try, two drop-goals, a penalty and two conversions as Gloucester beat second division champions Bedford to win the inaugural trophy.

He even managed to produce a try-saving tackle.

Man-of-the-match Mapletoft said: "We wanted revenge for when they came to Kingsholm and beat us.

"The try was nice because I've been a bit barren on the old try-scoring this year."

Three thousand Gloucester fans made the journey to Northampton's Franklin's Gardens and they were not disappointed as the silver trophy and £20,000 prize money headed back to the West Country with the Cherry and White army.

And so much did skipper Pete Glanville and his players value the mobile Shed that they even went on a lap of thanks before collecting the cup!

It was a very proud day for Hill, who had rushed up from London after the England A victory over Ireland to see what turned out to be a magnificent final.

They went 5-0 up as many minutes when top try scorer Terry Fanolua gathered up a bouncing Mapletoft cross-kick and raced in unopposed.

By Dave Barton
Gloucester 33
Bedford 25

Richard Ward collected the second try when he was mauled over after fellow lock Dave Sims had won the line-out.

Bedford came storming back and scrum-half Simon Crabb snapped-up the ball to burrow over.

Right-wing Ben Whetstone reduced the Gloucester lead with a drop-goal before Mapletoft restored the margin with a penalty and a drop kick of his own to take his team into an 18-8 half-time lead.

Junior Paramore almost collected Bedford's second try minutes after the break, following a burst down the flank but Mapletoft managed to cling to the Western Samoan's back and haul him into touch.

The Blues eventually clawed some points back when former Wales international full-back Mike Rayer kicked a penalty.

After six scrums in a row, which finally saw No 8 Simon Devereux held up before the line, they had another stab at it before referee Brian Campsall lost patience with Bedford and awarded a penalty try.

Campsall was even-handed by giving Bedford a penalty try minutes later for deliberate offside.

Brilliant

A brilliant piece of solo skill from Mapletoft put Gloucester 30-18 ahead when he chipped over the defence and dribbled to the line before pouncing for the touchdown.

And his drop goal made the result safe with three minutes of normal time left.

That just left time for Paramore to race away between the sticks to set up a nail-biting finish.

But a Fanolua try-saving tackle on former England wing Rory Underwood was the final act – and Gloucester started to party.

Gloucester: A Lumsden; R Jewell, T Fanolua, R Tombs, P Saint-Andre, M Mapletoft, I Benk; T Woodman (rep P Jones (8mins)), N McCarthy, A Deacon, R Ward (rep A Gibbs (68mins)), D Sims, P Glanville (capt), S Ojomoh, S Devereux. Reps not used I Sanders, M Kimber, C Fortey, A Hazell.

Scorers: Tries – Fanolua, Ward, pen try, Mapletoft, Pen – Mapletoft Cons – Mapletoft (2). Drop-goals – Mapletoft (2).

Bedford: M Rayer, B Whetstone, J Paramore, M Fetchley (temp S Breating 5-10 & 34-37mins), R Underwood, P Turner (capt), B Crabb; N Hatley, J Richards, C Boyd, S Murray, S Pugford, R Henders, J Forster, R Strauss. Reps not used Stone, A Davis, J Collins, D Hinkins, S Howard.

Scorers: Tries – Crabb, pen try Paramore, Pen – Rayer, Drop goal – Whetstone, Cons – Rayer (2)

Referee: B Campsall (Halifax)
Attendance: 6,000

CUP OF JOY . . . for Gloucester

U

UNIVERSITIES

The 1982/83 season was the last occasion when the Club played both Oxford and Cambridge Universities. Playing for Oxford on 30ᵗʰ October at Iffey Road was one Stuart Barnes. Gloucester put Oxford and Barnes to the sword in a 34-9 victory. Just four days later at Kingsholm the Light Blues were defeated 33-9. Guess who was playing for the Cambridge team at fly half – one Rob Andrew!

UNDEAFEATED

The first season the Club remained undefeated at Kingsholm was in the 1920-1921 campaign. They recorded 19 victories and drew 2 matches. Those nineteen wins came versus:

Lydney 17-0, Bath 9-6, Northampton 14-8, Cinderford 5-0, Bristol 6-3, Guy's Hospital 6-3, Moseley 29-0, Swansea 10-0, Stroud 24-0, Old Merchant Taylors 16-3, Bridgewater 18-8, Leicester 12-3, United Services 16-3, Newport 12-9, Cheltenham 18-9, Cardiff 16-11, Coventry 26-5, Llanelli 11-8, Manchester 20-3.

The two drawn matches were United Services 5-5 and Pontypool 5-5.

UNDEFEATED AGAIN

It was not until the 1971-72 season that the Club could claim a season where they remained undefeated at Kingsholm again. In that season they recorded 22 victories from 23 fixtures with one draw.

The twenty two victories were versus:

Clifton 26-11, Coventry 16-15, Ebbw Vale 16-12, Harlequins 12-4, Newport 18-0, Oxford University 16-6, Moseley 23-10, Lydney 14-3, Bath 24-16, Old Merchant Taylors 67-3, Wasps 28-3, Newbridge 16-6, St Lukes 23-14, Swansea 16-10, Aberavon 12-9, Richmond 17-0, Cheltenham 21-3, Guys Hospital 33-13, Headingly 18-6, Birkenhead Park 29-4, Stroud 16-6, Pontypool 16-4.

An almost impeccable record was spoilt by a 12-12 draw with Bristol in only the third home match of that season.

UNIVERSAL

The complete record was first achieved in 1981-82 when Steve Mills captained the Club to this elusive but enviable record. All 28 matches were won and they were versus:

Stroud 22-3, Coventry 21-15, Rosslyn Park 25-0, Pontypridd 16-12, Newbridge 6-0, Cheltenham 19-3, Pontypool 14-3, Ebbw Vale 23-0, Newport 19-0, Nottingham 20-7, Loughborough College 34-0, Oxford University 46-6, South Wales Police 24-4, Plymouth Albion 58-0, London Irish 19-6, Lydney 27-7, Moseley 27-21, High Wycombe 40-6, Bristol 10-3, Exeter 34-3, Sale 13-6, Saracens 30-12, Abertillery 21-7, Headingly 34-4, Birkenhead Park 24-12, Sale 40-0, Bath 33-15 and Exeter 21-7.

UNBEATEN

The Club's longest run of undefeated matches, 51 in total at Kingsholm, stretched from 10 December 1970 to 23rd September 1972.

In 2002-2003 season the Club were undefeated in 16 matches at Kingsholm. This was the least amount won in a team compared with other season achievements but it must be remembered in the professional era there is a reduced fixture list. These sixteen wins were versus:

Sale 44-8, Bristol 45-18, Saracens 44-14, Northampton 18-9, Leeds 28-10, London Irish 25-20, Wasps 24-17, Bath 29-16, Newcastle 25-23, Harlequins 29-11, Leicester 31-13, Munster 35-16, Perpignan 33-16, Viadana 64-16, Exeter 35-6 and Saracens 51-20.

UP UNTIL

Up until 1960 only two players had amassed 150 points in a season for the Club. They were Willie Jones who passed the 200 points mark mainly due to 174 points obtained from drop goals, and Tom Millington whose 161 points in the 1921/1922 season was the previous record.

UMPIRES

In the early days of the Club's history, Club captains were often their teams umpires as there we were no referees as we know them. It was not surprising that such items as a disputed goal or try frequently appeared on the same sheets! As public interest increased each side appointed an umpire but this did not prove satisfactory and in the early 1880s referees were appointed for important matches. They had nothing to do with the conduct of the game but simply strolled along the touchline and when the umpires came to a deadlock they heard both sides then gave their decision.

As the game became faster and more open, this system slowed the game down. So in 1885 the referee was given a whistle and appeared in the middle of the field of play but had limited powers. Umpires carrying flags still followed the game and referees were unable to grant any appeal until at least one of the them raised his stick!

Umpires turned into touch judges and the referee received appeals directly from players and adjudicated at once. Later it was agreed to leave the whole conduct of the game in his hands so that an 'appeal' disappeared from the Rugby Union laws.

UNOFFICIAL

Three players won International caps for England in the Second World War – Tom Price, Gordon Hudson and John Thornton.

UNBEATEN CAPTAIN – 1920/21

The Club captain in that undefeated season was Fred Webb.

UNDEFEATED BY ENGLISH TEAMS

Unbeaten in the 1900/1901 season was Gloucester's record versus all England teams.

UNITED STATES OF AMERICA

The U.S.A. Rugby Tournament held in Boston at the conclusion of the 1991/1992 season saw victories obtained versus Washington (USA) 28-12 and Vancouver (Canada) 23-0.

OPPONENTS – U

Opponents have been: University of Pennsylvania, United Services, United Services (Portsmouth), University Athletic Union, U.C.S. Old Boys and Ulster.

UNITED

Gloucester United in 1973/74 season became the first side in Gloucester R.F.C.'s history to put three figures on the scoreboard when they recorded a 103 points to three victory against Hereford in September 1973. The most points recorded by a United XV came in the previous season of 1972/73 when they totalled 1,202 points. In 1911/12 season the United team were credited with 24 tries when they played Stow-on-the-Wold R.F.C.

UNIVERSITY COSTS

When Cambridge University visited Kingsholm to meet Gloucester R.F.C. on 25th January 1975 the programme cost 5 pence. When Oxford University visited likewise on 29th October 1983 the cost of the Club programme was 20 pence.

V

VERNON PUGH

Vernon Pugh who led the International Rugby Board announced on 25 August 1995 that the game would become 'open'. It was on 4 March 1996 that all clubs, including Gloucester, could sign players on professional contracts.

VOYCE IN 150TH

Tom Voyce, the Gloucester Rugby Football Club flanker played in England's 150th International match played at Cardiff Arms Park on 16th January 1926 against Wales in a three points apiece drawn match.

VERSATILE

Tom Voyce who played as a forward for Gloucester, England and the British Lions originally played at centre. However, when he went for England trials he was put down for the forwards. Tom's versatility was well documented on the injury hit Lions tour of 1924 when he played as a wing three quarter and full back.

VOYCE ONE OF THE EIGHT

Tom Voyce was one of eight England Internationals to have scored tries against each of the other four countries in the old Five Nations Championship.

VICTORIES

The most victories recorded in a season was in the 1981/82 campaign when 41 matches were won. Steve Mills was the Club Captain that season. That total came from 48 matches played.

VIDEO REPLAY

The first time Gloucester supporters saw Rugby entering a new technology era was in 2000 with the introduction of the video replay as to whether a try had been scored.

THE VOLCANO

Tongan born Lesley Vainikolo made the most remarkable Premiership debut ever when he scored five tries on his debut versus Leeds Carnegie on 16th September 2007. Lesley joined Gloucester Rugby Club from Rugby League club Bradford Bulls where he had scored 149 tries in 152 appearances. Within five months of his Rugby Union debut he was capped by England versus Wales on 2nd February 2008.

OPPONENTS – V

Vaal Triangle (South Africa) and Viadana (Italy).

VOYCE

Tom Voyce was a legendary figure in the rugby world for over 50 years from the time he became a schoolboy International through his playing days as an outstanding forward and then various administrative posts. He was R.F.U. President in 1960-61 although due to retire finally from the Rugby Football Union at the Annual General Meeting of 1970, under the rule that only 'the most recent eight living ex-presidents may continue to serve'. He was co-opted for a further year to complete a half century of service to the R.F.U. as a player, committee man and President.

Tom played in the match to celebrate the Centenary of Rugby in 1923 which took place at Rugby School Close when playing for a combined England and Wales team that defeated Scotland and Ireland. With 15 minutes to go the score was level at 15 points each. Tom decided the issue by scoring the winning try which was duly converted. He was a member of the England teams of 1921, 1923 and 1924 which gained the Triple Crown.

VOYCE AT EASTER

Tom Voyce, the former Gloucester and England back row forward played in three International matches playing on an Easter Monday in 1921, 1923 and 1925 at Stade Colombes Paris.

PHIL VICKERY

Phil Vickery is the Club's most capped player. He was awarded 47 International Caps by England in his Kingsholm career.

VOYCE IN SUCCESSION

Tom Voyce made 27 consecutive International appearances for England between 1920 and 1926.

VIOLENCE

The season of 1922/23 was the Club's most violent season with a total of 28 players dismissed from the field. Fourteen for fighting, six for obscene language, one for foul play and seven for arguing with the referee.

NO TO VIOLENCE

In the 1922/23 season Leicester declined to play fixtures with Gloucester because of violent play.

NATIONAL CUP WINNER

Brian Vine   1978

A VOYCE AMONG LIONS

Tommy Voyce played twice for the British Lions on their tour to South Africa in 1925. He later became President of the Rugby Football Union and was awarded an O.B.E.

VICTORIES

A total of 50 consecutive victories at Kingsholm were celebrated in 1972.

'V' FOR ENGLAND

Two players with their surname beginning with 'V' have represented England – Phil Vickery and Tom Voyce.

A TRIO

Opponents have been: Vaal Triangle (South Africa), Vancouver (Canada) and Viadana.

AN EVER-PRESENT VOYCE

Tom Voyce of Gloucester Rugby Football Club played in all four of England's International matches of 1921 when they won the Five Nations Championship, Triple Crown and the Grand Slam. They repeated the feat in 1924 when once again Tom Voyce was ever present.

VICKERY IN RECORD

Phil Vickery was a member of the England team that recorded a 60-26 win over Wales at Twickenham on 21st February 1998 to set a new record for the highest score in a championship match.

VIDEOS

'Cherry and White' supporters have been able to purchase two videos that brought great delight to their fanatical fans: *And Bath Came Second*, and *Gloucester Glory* following the Powergen Cup story of 2003.

W

NO BARRIERS FOR WINDO

Former Gloucester prop forward, Tony Windo, who departed from Kingsholm in 1999, was not only the Guinness Partnership's oldest surviving Englishman before he retired in 2008; he was also the only player to be playing in the Division who was born in the 1960s. The Gloucester born, loose head prop forward was born in 1969. Tony made his 100th Premiership appearance versus Bristol on 3rd May 2008. The indefatigable Worcester loose head made these appearances for Gloucester while at Kingsholm.

	Appearances	Tries	Points
National League	62 + 3	7	35
National Cup	5 + 1	1	5
European Shield	9	2	10
TOTALS	76 + 4	10	50

WELSH INTERNATIONALS

Players who have been capped by Wales while members of Gloucester R.F.C. are John Gwilliam (1952-53) who made 50 appearances for the Club, scoring 4 tries.

Gareth Delve who joined the Club from Bath R.F.C. in 2007 and Will James who moved to Kingsholm from Exeter. Gareth Cooper became the second former Bath player to be capped by the Principality while on the Kingsholm playing staff.

NATIONAL CUP WINNERS – W

John Watkins	1972, 1978
Chris Williams	1978
Paul Wood	1982
Trevor Woodman	2003
Viv Wooley	1978

ONE OF THREE FOR THE WORLD CUP

Kingsholm was one of only three club venues to host a World Cup match in 1991. The match held there was between New Zealand and the U.S.A. Eagles.

FORMER WELSH INTERNATIONALS TO MOVE TO KINGSHOLM

Former Ebbw Vale players Byron Hayward and Kingsley Jones had appeared for Wales before joining the Kingsholm playing staff. In fact Kingsley Jones had captained Wales as had John Gwilliam in the 1950s. Gareth Cooper, the former Bath and Newport Gwent Dragon had also previously represented Wales, as had Gareth Delve.

WARTIME INTERNATIONALS

Gordon Hudson (son of Arthur) and Grahame Parker both played in the Scotland versus England match at Inverleith.

In the wartime match at Kingsholm between England and Wales, Francis Edwards, having played for Broughton Park and Leicester after leaving Gloucester in 1928 appeared for the home country.

Tom Price and Gordon Hudson both played in the victory International of 1945-6 against the New Zealand Kiwis. Johnny Thornton replaced Gordon Hudson for the matches against Wales, Scotland and Ireland.

WIELDING INFLUENCE

Tom Walkinshaw was unveiled as the Club's first owner when he purchased a 73 per cent stake on 29th April 1997. He was 50 years of age.

WORCESTER STREET

The Worcester Street stand was erected in 1954 with concrete terracing added in the same year.

WORLD CUP

Two Gloucester players, both prop forwards, appeared in England's World Cup Final winning team of 2003 – Philip Vickery and Trevor Woodman.

FIRST WELSH

The first Welsh club to provide the opposition was Newport in 1878.

WALES IN ABUNDANCE

In the season of 1888/89 ten of the Club's fixtures were played versus Welsh clubs, four of those against Cardiff.

DEFEAT FOR THE WELSH

The top four Welsh clubs, Cardiff, Newport, Swansea and Llanelli were defeated for the first time in the 1899/1900 season. This prompted the Club to have a reputation for excessively violent play and the team being reported as a 'big, lusty and vigorous lot'.

FRED WADLEY

Club Captain, Fred Wadley played in every 1st XV fixture for two consecutive seasons in 1935/36 and 1936/37.

SIX WITH W

Six players with their surname beginning with 'W' have played for England: Richard West, Chris Williams, Ken Wilson, Alf Wood, Trevor Woodman and John Watkins.

OPPONENTS – W

Opponents have been: Wakefield, Walsall, Washington (U.S.A.), Wasps, Watsonians, Waterloo, Welsh Army, Welsh Universities, West Hartlepool, Weston-Super-Mare, Wigan, Wolfhounds, Worcester and Wolverhampton.

SEVEN FOR WOOD

Former Gloucester full back Alf Wood was capped three times by England at Rugby Union, 4 times by Great Britain at Rugby League.

TOM WALKINSHAW

When Tom Walkinshaw purchased the Club he was Chairman of TWR Group, which was established in 1976. Also an owner, Chairman and Team Principal of the now defunct Arrows Grand Prix International Racing Team.

TWR's business was the design, engineering an manufacturing of road and racing cars and road and racing engines.

Tom, was born in 1947, and was the son of a Scottish farmer. He entered motor racing as a driver in 1968. He was a successful driver with several victories. He decided to retire and concentrate on the Jaguar Sportscar Programme that TWR ran for six years, winning Le Mans twice and the World Championship three times.

At one period his company employed 1,500 working in the United Kingdom, Sweden, Australia, New Zealand and the United States. Cars such as the Aston Martin DB7 and the Volvo C70 established Tom Walkinshaw at the forefront of the automotive world.

In 1997, Tom, was voted 'Autocar Man of the Year'. His private interest apart from the Rugby Club include skiing and shooting. In 2008 he decided to sell some of his shareholding in the Club to Martin St Quinton.

X

XMAS

Yuletide was a favourite time of the year for Rugby Clubs in the amateur era. Clubs would play fixtures on Christmas Day and Boxing Day. Old Merchant Taylors and University Athletic Union were the statutory fixtures for season after season.

The only season where we restricted both clubs from recording any points was in the 1955-56 season when Peter Ford was the Club Captain. Old Merchant Taylors were defeated 22-0 on Christmas Day and University Athletic Union by an identical score line on Boxing Day.

A scale model of the home stadium, on display at Kingsholm

Y

DIMITRI YACHVILI

Dimitri Yachvili, the Biarritz scrum half who also played in the Gloucester team of the early years of this century is one of 12 players who have scored 50 or more points against England in International matches. To date he has scored 53 points. Dimitri kicked six penalties against England for France at Twickenham on 13th February 2005 enabling 'Le Bleus' to record a one point win by 18 points to seventeen.

YELLOW CARDS

We received more disciplinary cards on the calendar year of 2006 than we had in any year since the game of Rugby Union went professional. Those who received the 10 minute break were as follows:

Mike Tindall	Bayonne	Home
Patrice Collazo	Leicester	Home
Peter Buxton	Northampton	Away
Mike Tindall	Sale	Away
Ryan Lamb	Worcester	Home
Alex Brown	Leeds	Away
Mark Foster	Ospreys	Away
Patrice Collazo	Bristol	Home
Peter Buxton	Worcester	Away
James Forrester	Worcester	Away
James Bailey	Saracens	Home
Alex Brown	Wasps	Home
Mike Tindall	Edinburgh	Home
Willie Walker	Edinburgh	Away
Carlos Neito	Wasps	Away

In other calendar years since the Millennium the figures relating to yellow cards read as: 2002 – 7, 2003 – 2, 2004 – 7, 2005 – 6, and 2007 – 13.

In 2008 the 'Cherry and Whites', surpassed all records for the Club albeit in a disciplinary manner.

A. Hazell	Saracens – Away	R. Lamb	London Irish – Away
P. Buxton	Wasps – Away	C. Nieto	Ospreys – Home
A. Hazell	Harlequins – Home	M. Bortolami	Bristol – Home
P. Buxton	Ospreys – Away	L. Narraway	Ospreys – Away
O. Azam	Ospreys – Away	A. Qera	Ulster – Home
R. Lamb	Wasps – Home	W. James	Leicester – Home
A. James	Leicester – Home	M. Bortolami	Bristol – Away
O. Azam	London Irish – Home	D. Tuohy	Sale – Away
C. Neito	Munster – Home	W. James	Leeds – Home
M. Bortolami	Leeds – Home	C. Nieto	Wasps – Away

View from the stands during the build up to a 2007 fixture

Z

ZURICH CHAMPIONSHIP FINAL

The Zurich Championship Final on 8th June 2002 saw Gloucester Rugby defeat Bristol Shoguns at Twickenham by 28 points to 23 in front of an attendance of 28,500, the first trophy success for 20 years.

The match day programme cost £4.00 and the Bristol Director of Rugby was Dean Ryan, later to move to Kingsholm as Head Coach.

ZURICH PREMIERSHIP FINAL

In the Zurich Premiership Final at Twickenham on 31st May 2003 Gloucester were heavily defeated by London Wasps. The team was:

Thinus Delport; Marcel Garvey, Terry Fanolua, Henry Paul, James Simpson-Daniel; Ludovic Mercier, Andy Gomarsall; Rodrigo Roncero, Olivier Azam, Phil Vickery (Captain), Adam Eustace, Mark Cornwall, Jake Boer, Andy Hazell and Junior Paramore.

Replacements: Clive Stuart Smith, Robert Todd, Simon Amor, Rob Fidler and Peter Buxton.

The match day programme cost £4.00.
A seat in the East Middle Stand cost £25.00.

1

1 MILLION SPECTATORS AT KINGSHOLM

It was announced on 17th May 2002 that the forthcoming Zurich Championship Quarter Final match between Gloucester and Newcastle Falcons would attract the one millionth supporter for Zurich matches and they would turn up at the turnstiles to a match at Kingsholm on 18th May 2002.

Construction of the Buildbase stand

Cup triumph for Gloucester

by Katie Coker

Gloucester 33, Bedford 25

GLOUCESTER ended a 20-year 15-a-side trophy drought by winning the Cheltenham and Gloucester Cup.

Incisive attacking, and endless amounts of gritty defence enabled them to take the trophy, to the utter delight of the thousands of fans who were there to cheer them on.

Anyone who thought this competition was worthless should have been at Franklin's Gardens for the final.

The crowd of 6000 was in full voice in support of both teams throughout, the rugby was as fast and furious as you will see and there was no doubt about the will to win of both teams.

Gloucester coach John Brain had said the first 20 minutes would be crucial. He could not have wanted to see his team defend for almost that entire time, but even though they were forced to do so, Gloucester still came out of that period 12-0 up.

Bedford became forced to defend from the outset and came desperately close to scoring several times. However, Gloucester defended with their hearts and souls as well as their bodies and held them out.

With six minutes gone, Dave Sims stole a Bedford line-out at around half-way and powered up the wing.

Andy Deacon took the ball on, Laurie Beck found Mark Mapletoft and the fly-half put up a high, cross-field kick.

Terry Fanolua collected the loose ball and raced in on the left for a try which Mapletoft failed to convert.

Bedford were straight back on the attack, Gloucester cleared their lines several times, only to put themselves back under pressure with infringements or errors.

However, Gloucester's defence was equal to the task again and after 22 minutes they scored their second try. Gloucester attacked from a free-kick and forced a line-out in the left corner when Bedford fumbled a Mapletoft grubber kick.

Sims caught Neil McCarthy's throw and Gloucester drove swiftly for the line, where Richard Ward touched down for a try which Mapletoft converted.

Steve Ojomoh halted a dangerous run from Junior Paramore and Simon Crabb wasted a good chance when he knocked-on a tapped penalty close to Gloucester's line.

Fanolua was then called upon to make a try-saving tackle on his cousin Paramore and Ojomoh and Richard Tombs forced Rudi Straeuli into touch right in the left-hand corner.

However, that good work was wasted when Sims lost the subsequent line-out, and Crabb darted in for a try which Rayer failed to convert.

Ben Whetstone kicked a 33rd minute drop-goal for Bedford, but Gloucester swept back into the opposition's half with a break by Saint-Andre and when Bedford were penalised for offside, Mapletoft kicked a 37th minute penalty.

A break by Simon Devereux put Gloucester back on

■ Richard Ward ran in a try for Gloucester during their 33-25 C and G Cup final win.

the attack and Mapletoft kicked a drop-goal on the stroke of half-time to go into the break with an 18-8 lead.

Paramore almost claimed a try early in the second half, but he was stopped at the last second. However, Rayer kicked a penalty for Bedford eight minutes into the half.

A long touch kick from Mapletoft and a line-out steal by Gloucester set up almost 10 minutes of pressure on the Bedford line. Gloucester had eight scrums – many of which they opted for from penalties – and eventually Brian Campsall awarded a penalty try in the 19th minute which Mapletoft converted to stretch the lead to 25-11.

Bedford forced an immediate line-out on the Gloucester line and Gloucester eventually conceded a penalty try as Paul Turner took a quick tap and Gloucester infringed for the umpteenth time. There was a quick fight, which resulted in a talking-to for

Sims, and Rayer converted the try.

Just three minutes after Bedford's try, Mapletoft put a trademark chip and chase over the defence to score a try, but his conversion missed.

After more defending from Gloucester, Mapletoft kicked a 37th minute drop-goal, but a minute later Paramore raced in for a breakaway try under the posts, which Rayer converted.

That set up a tense finale, but one minute into injury time, Fanolua made a try-saving tackle on Rory Underwood, and it was all over.

GLOUCESTER: A. Lumsden; R. Jewell, T. Fanolua, R. Tombs, P. Saint Andre; M. Mapletoft, L. Beck; T. Woodman, N. McCarthy, A. Deacon, R. Ward (A. Gibbs, 70 min), D. Sims, S. Ojomoh, P. Glanville (capt), S. Devereux. Other reps. I. Sanders, M. Kimber, P. Jones. C. Fortey, A. Hazell.

BEDFORD: M. Rayer; B. Whetstone, J. Paramore, M. Pechey (S. Brading, temp rep), R. Underwood; P. Turner, S. Crabb; N. Hatley, J. Richards, C. Boyd, S. Murray, S. Platford, R. Winters, J. Forster, R. Straeuli. Other reps: R. Stone, A. Davis, J. Cullen, D. Hinkins, S. Howard.

REFEREE: Brian Campsall (Yorkshire Society).

Six-try England see off the Irish

England A 40, Ireland A 30

ENGLAND A ran in six tries to demolish the Irish and end a six-match losing run.

Spencer Brown and Ben Sturnham scored a try apiece to give England a 15-0 lead and a handy platform to combat Ireland's mid-match revival. Tim Stimpson kicked a penalty and conversion.

Once Ireland entered the scoring action at the start of the second quarter they were full value, with stand-off Barry Everitt and centre

Mervyn Murphy working productively in midfield.

Niall Woods collected a penalty in the 20th minute before his team scored two tries in three minutes to go ahead at 17-15.

Everitt's break allowed Murphy to score and Murphy then put wing John McWeeney in. Woods converted both scores.

Stimpson's penalty gave England an 18-17 interval lead and England swept away with four tries in 13 minutes.

Peter Mensah cut through Ireland's defence and Gloucester lock Rob Fidler crashed over, with Stimpson converting.

Mensah intercepted a pass on halfway and sprinted away to score. England's other lock Craig Gillies finished off an all-Richmond move and Lewsey followed up a bouncing ball to take England to 40.

Woods interrupted England's sequence with a couple of penalties and converted Everitt's late try.

Glorious Gloucester keep the flag flying

Gloucester	40
Northampton	22

PAUL ACKFORD
AT TWICKENHAM

First Lansdowne Road, now Twickenham, English rugby is going through the purplest of purple patches at the moment. This was another tremendous occasion played out in blinding sunshine in front of two fervent and marvellously partisan sets of supporters. Gloucester were deserved winners, powered home by James Simpson-Daniel and inspired by James Forrester. Behind at half-time, they surged back with a wonderful second-half performance of almost total dominance to send Northampton to their third Twickenham defeat in four years.

But, as important, it was another great day for the sport and another reason why the bigwigs of the International Rugby Board should give the 2007 World Cup to England when they vote in Dublin on Wednesday. If the English rugby public can get this excited over a club final heaven knows how they would respond if the World Cup came to town.

Most of the pre-match questions were aimed at Northampton. Savaged in last year's final by London Irish, it was unthinkable that they could capitulate again. Coach Wayne Smith designated two captains to lead them on to the pitch. "I want John Leslie and Budge Pountney to share in the responsibility of the final," Smith said. It was as if one man could not shoulder the burden alone.

And at the start of a tumultuous and turbulent first half it appeared as if the responsibility was too much even for two men. Northampton scored first through a Paul Grayson penalty but it was Gloucester who rattled the cage the hardest. At the restart, Gloucester's forwards drove ferociously, forcing Matt Dawson to fire a pass intended for Steve Thompson into no-man's-land where the swooping Simpson-Daniel snapped up the ball and strolled over for the try. When Ludovic Mercier added the conversion and a dropped goal six minutes later the prospect of another Northampton crumble was on.

But Northampton responded in a manner befitting a team comprising 14 internationals. North Harbour lock Matt Lord was their only non Test player, and he Dawson, Budge Pountney, Thompson and Ben Cohen combined to stabilise Northampton.

Grayson was just as influential in the early stages. He finished the half with 17 points and it was his break inside Mercier that set up the try for Nick Beal. Grayson is under intense scrutiny as the understudy to Jonny Wilkinson, but his early play when he mixed up his options was shrewd and accurate. And it would be foolish to make too much of the moment when he hauled down Mercier before the ball had arrived. Grayson was sent to the sin bin for that offence and the resultant penalty gave Gloucester an important lead at 30-22 going into the last quarter, but that aberration coincided with a spell during which Northampton could not put together an attack worthy of the name.

It was typical of the occasion and of the new-look Gloucester that they struck late in the first half through Marcel Garvey to get back into the match and were first to score after the break to edge ahead of Northampton. There was a time when Gloucester could not win away and one of the fears for them yesterday was that they would be unable to repeat their Kingsholm form. That concern was heightened after 21 minutes when Rob Fidler was sent to the sin bin for talking back to the referee. Tony Spreadbury, but it is a mark of Gloucester's inner strength that they shrugged off Fidler's absence and regained the lead early in the second half.

Once again it was Forrester who produced the decisive move. Northampton made a mess of their scrummage when Andrew Blowers was caught and Gloucester moved the ball right for the indecently quick Forrester to canter over in the corner. There was more than a hint of controversy to the score because television replays seemed to show that the Gloucester flanker did not have contact with the ball in the act of touching it down but none of the officials spotted it.

It was a good afternoon for Forrester, who has made startling progress up the rankings. He has presence and has shown that he does not fade on the big occasion. Henry Paul was another to tickle the England selectors' fancies. The mastermind of England's sensational Hong Kong Sevens triumph, Paul was very tidy in the centre against Northampton.

That, in essence, was the difference between the two sides. Gloucester do not have the seasoned performers which Northampton can call upon. Bar a couple of oldies they are an outfit making their way in the game and it was Gloucester's collective energy and desire which finally did for Northampton.

It was no coincidence that the final *coup de théâtre* occurred when Dawson, attempting to make something out of nothing and save the game, was intercepted by Mercier who found the flying Simpson-Daniel. Two big matches in a week was too much for Dawson and his England colleagues. All Gloucester were worried about was winning one game. They did and in some style.

Day tripper... Northampton's Ben Cohen is upended by Ludovic Mercier of Gloucester at Twickenham yesterday / *Jamie McDonald*

Fine first year draws to an end for Fanolua

by **Katie Coker**
rugby writer

WHEN Richard Hill signed players from around the globe last summer to strengthen his Gloucester squad, everyone at the club knew it might be tough for the recruits to settle into their new environment.

But they have made themselves at home in Gloucester and have been accepted by their team-mates and the supporters.

Philippe Saint-André was the biggest name among the recruits, but the two who have attracted the most attention in the last few weeks are the centre pairing of Richard Tombs and Terry Fanolua.

They have now played 31 and 28 first team games respectively and their partnership is earning praise from players, coaches and pundits around the country.

When they signed for Gloucester, Tombs – an Australian – billed himself as a creator of tries rather than a prolific scorer and it soon became clear that Fanolua – from Western Samoa – was the fastest player in the club and a potentially lethal finisher.

Fanolua (23) arrived in England alone, having never been away from his family home in New Zealand for more than two months. He took a while to find his feet, but he was welcomed by his team-mates and is certainly enjoying his stay in Gloucester – despite occasional homesickness.

A big concern for the Western Samoan international in the autumn was his failure to score a try in the first few matches.

He finally broke his duck in his 10th game – the 29-7 win over London Irish in the Premiership on October 19.

Since then, he has barely looked back and has now scored a total of 12 tries in the 28 games he has played. He and Tombs are being lauded as one of the top centre partnerships in English rugby and Fanolua is certainly enjoying himself.

"Everything has gone really well. Everyone has been great – I have had no problems," said Fanolua, who shared a house with Phil Vickery and Trevor Woodman before moving into his own flat in Gloucester a few months ago.

"At first I found it hard to settle in. I was a bit homesick. But after a while I got to know the boys and they are really good.

"They got me involved and I have settled in well.

"The best part about my being here is the guys – the players. They have been really, really good to me.

"I get along with everybody. There are no egos in the team, everyone is down to earth and they make me laugh.

"The crowd and the Shed are unbelievable. They are one of the best crowds I have played in front of. It is an awesome atmosphere at Kingsholm.

"The most difficult part about being here is missing home. I have got a baby daughter and I miss her. I went home for her first birthday in February."

The passion of the players and supporters has impressed Fanolua and he

■ Terry Fanolua on the ball for Gloucester at Kingsholm.

is enthusiastic about the club and hopes to serve Gloucester even better next season.

"Tombsy [Richard Tombs] is a top guy. He has helped me a lot with my game. I have enjoyed playing next to him," he said. "Our partnership has become pretty good and we will be looking to improve on that and keep it going for the remainder of our stay here.

"The standard of the matches has been really strong. It is pretty hard and it is a long season – and boy it takes its toll.

"There are no easy games. All the guys I have played have been impressive."

Fanolua has been playing rugby almost constantly for two years and he will have little chance to rest this summer. On May 19 he flies south for a summer of rugby with Samoa and will not be back at Kingsholm until late September.

'Kingsholm talK'

DIRECTOR of coaching **Richard Hill** on his Gloucester team's defeat at Harlequins last Sunday:

"I had a gut feeling that we would win. It was nothing objective – it was very subjective.

"We all appreciate that for Gloucester to take the next step from being a mid-table club, we need to win away from home.

"We have a massive challenge ahead of us. I was optimistic that we could do it at the first time of asking, but life isn't as easy as that.

"We lose a bit of impetus in the second half. We will have to experiment with going out onto the pitch at half-time to do some more preparation."

GLOUCESTER centre **Terry Fanolua** on the team's recent performances:

"For the last two matches I haven't been in it much and a few of the boys reckon we have stuck with the forwards too much rather than spreading the ball out.

"We have got a great bunch of forwards – perhaps the best pack in the country.

"But some players are over used and we are not using the pace of the back line.

"We have got moves we practice in training all week and then we don't use them.

"It is something we should be looking to change, and we are looking to do that.

"We have been playing too much nine man rugby instead of 15 man rugby."

HILL'S aims for the remainder of this season:

"A top four finish is not top of our priority list. Beating either Northampton or Richmond away is the top priority.

"I don't want to leave this away match thing lingering on."

Gloucester happy with Italian job

By Barrie Fairall

TREVISO	12
GLOUCESTER	33

UNITED in cherry and white, Gloucester showed their true colours in Italy with a satisfying performance at the home of Benetton.

While Treviso were no pushovers, by the finish they had been squeezed for four tries that left Nigel Melville's men celebrating a job well done, thanks to pocketing a bonus point.

At the start of their European journey the point was a useful acquisition for Gloucester. Mighty Munster sit waiting in Pool Five and next up come the French side Bourgoin, so a late touchdown from Adam Eustace was worth a pint or two in the hostelries on Saturday.

"It was a good start," Melville, Gloucester's director of rugby, said. "They were a well-coached outfit with a strong pack. They may have lived off scraps, but you get them on a muddy day at Kingsholm and they'll take some beating. That bonus point could prove useful." While Gloucester pressed in the early stages, turnovers robbed them of scoring chances.

That was frustrating as Treviso were able to weather the storm with no hint of panic. Better still for local supporters, they struck first to set the match alight, by catching Gloucester on the back foot.

Attacking off a line-out, the South African fly-half Franco Smith cut neatly between Henry Paul and Duncan McRae. The breach made, Tommaso Visentin raced over, and there was more to come from this Treviso side coached by former All Black wing Craig Green.

If Gloucester – with Thinus Delport in the sin-bin – thought that a tremendous long-range strike from the flying wing James Simpson-Daniel had their opponents on the run, they were mistaken. Next up came a hack-on try by Gonzalo Canale.

Suitably chastened, Gloucester now stirred themselves without further reply. Junior Paramore, the man of the match, twice made it to the line, Paul landed two more penalties and Eustace had the last say with a 25-yard gallop for that bonus point.